THE EAST INDIA COMPANY

*The title page of the 1712 Journal of Isaac Pike, Captain of the Stringer,
showing the East India Company defending its trading monopoly in the East.*

THE
EAST INDIA
COMPANY

TRADE AND CONQUEST FROM 1600

ANTONY WILD

HarperCollins*Illustrated* London

HarperCollins*Publishers* India

Special thanks to Air India for their help in facilitating this publication

First published in 1999 by HarperCollins*Illustrated*
an imprint of HarperCollins*Publishers*
77-85 Fulham Palace Road
London W6 8JB

and HarperCollins*Publishers* India Pvt Ltd
7/16 Ansari Road, Daryaganj, New Delhi 110 002

The HarperCollins website address is:
www.**fire**and**water**.com

Text © Antony Wild 1999
Photographs pages 72 (top & bottom), 169 © Antonio Martinelli; pages 14, 65
(bottom), 66 (top & bottom), 71, 76, 77, 172 (top), 174 © Museum of London;
page 49 © National Gallery, London; page 47 © National Trust Library/Mark Fiennes;
page 68 © The Dean and Chapter of Westminster; page 134 (right) © The Board and
Trustees of the Armouries (XXVIA.102); page 155 © Dr Oliver Impey

A CIP catalogue record for this book is available from the British Library

ISBN: 0 00 414054 0

Cartography: Martin Brown
Copy Editor: Caroline Taylor
Indexer: Sue Bosanko

99 01 03 02 00
2 4 6 8 9 7 5 3 1

Colour reproduction by Colourscan Pte. Ltd
Printed and bound in Great Britain by Bath Press Colourbooks

CONTENTS

CONTENTS AND CHRONOLOGY

DEFINITIONS, POLICIES, APOLOGIES & ACKNOWLEDGEMENTS

The Company which is the subject of this book was officially chartered by Queen Elizabeth I in 1600, as 'The Governor and Company of Merchants of London trading into the East Indies'. In 1709, it merged with another company trading to the East to form 'The United Company of Merchants of England trading to the East Indies'. Legally, this remained the official company name until 1874, but the Charter Act of 1833 referred to the company as 'The East India Company'. Although the official title was never rescinded, thereafter this term was used in Acts of Parliament, documents, contracts, etc. 'The East India Company' was also called 'The Honourable Company', 'John Company' (possibly derived from 'jehan', or 'powerful', as in Shah Jehan or Jehangir), or simply 'The Company'. The India Act of 1858 saw the end of the Company as an active entity, but the winding up process was not finally accomplished until 1874, when its last Charter expired.

The term 'servants' in connection with the Company, means any of its employees, from the Governor General to the lowliest clerk. Elsewhere, the term is used conventionally.

In defiance of current practice, text and map place names are those in use at the time of the late Company era.

By and large, the images used in this book predate 1858, but some stray beyond that year; I have tried where possible to ensure that in such instances the subjects of the pictures had not altered significantly in style or substance since 1858.

In India, and in the more politically sensitive of western texts, the disturbance in India in 1857 is usually called the 'First War of Independence'. Here, with due apologies, it is termed 'the Mutiny'.

The term 'the English' includes – again with due apologies – the Scots, the Irish and the Welsh; the term 'the British' is used in relation to subjects of the Crown, as distinct from servants of the Company.

The term 'raj' has come to be associated with British rule in India between the Company's demise in 1857 and Independence in 1947 ('the Raj'); here it is used in the general sense of 'rule'. Hence the 'Company's raj' refers to the period of the Company's domination of most or major parts of India until 1858.

Hobson-Jobson is the masterly glossary of Anglo-Indian words and phrases by H Yule and A C Burnell, first published in 1886.

This book covers over two hundred and fifty years and touches five continents: it contains little original research, as virtually every aspect of the Company's history has been covered minutely (and in separate volumes) by a number of historians over the years. What I have attempted to do, however, is to weave together the threads of their specialist knowledge into a general whole. My scavenging has left the half-digested fruits of their own original research scattered throughout the text; I can only hope that they do not feel disgraced by their unacknowledged association with this book. To them I owe the greatest debt.

Particular thanks are due to Polly Powell at HarperCollins who championed this work while it was only a twinkle in my eye, and to Fiona Screen, who had the unenviable task of making sense of it.

Others mentioned in dispatches are Jasper Brown, Vinod Dua, Deccan Aviation, Nina Rishad Escarzaga, Anthony Farrington, Cyrille and Diana de Gunzburg, Barbara and Rishad Khan, Antonio Martinelli, Oliver and Kitten Musker, and Arjun and Mila Oberoi.

I must also thank Hector and Girl who forewent their customary walks to look upon my work, and despair.

Civil Lines, Delhi 1999.

ORIGINS

> *'Our king has all the Indies in his arms,*
> *And more richer, when he strains that lady.'*
> Shakespeare, *Henry VIII*, 4.i.45

I n the high Himalayas of Tibet lies Lake Manasarowar, sacred to Hindus and Buddhists alike, from which four great rivers of the subcontinent are traditionally supposed to have emerged. One, the Indus, eventually bursts out onto the plains of what is now Pakistan and makes its way to the Arabian Sea; its valley was once home to an ancient civilisation comparable in sophistication to those of Egypt and Mesopotamia. In Sanskrit, the river was called 'Sindhu'– literally, 'the sea'– and a province on its banks still bears a like name. The sibilant 's' changed to an aspirant 'h' in Persian and, as variants of 'Hindu', the description of the river and the vast and mysterious country beyond it passed into Latin and Greek.

So vague was the understanding of where this country was that in the Dark Ages the name (in its newer form, 'India') was applied broadly to all Asia; this vast area was later also represented in the plural form, 'Indies', in European languages. In the fifteenth century, Columbus extended the meaning by naming his new discoveries in the Caribbean the 'West Indies', probably hoping thereby to deflect attention from the failure of his expedition to find a route to the (East) Indies. Native Americans from Alaska to Tierra del Fuego soon after became known as Indians, with the strange result that, in order to avoid confusion, centuries later the British in India ceased to apply the term 'Indian' to the natives of that land.

The expansion of European trade eastwards had led to the formation of various national incorporated companies, all including the local version of the term 'Indies' in their names. The Charter of the English East India Company, granted in 1600, gave it a monopoly on all English trade to

The Company's China fleet at anchor in the Straits of Sunda, between Java and Sumatra.

the east of the Cape of Good Hope. That such a definition could be stretched to encompass the entire globe – the Cape of Good Hope is, after all, but a long voyage east of the Cape of Good Hope – did not occur to those who drafted the Charter. One hundred and eighty years later the Company could be found trading as far east as Vancouver in the American Northwest, buying furs (with, one hopes, a due sense of linguistic irony) from the Indians there. At the beginning of the nineteenth century it was this East India Company which gave William Moorcroft, a veterinary surgeon in its service, permission to explore the mountains of Tibet. In 1811, Moorcroft was able to establish for the first time that the source of the river Indus, and of all these semantic difficulties, was not in fact Lake Manasarowar.

The Company's influence spread around the globe, its actions precipitating, directly or indirectly, such distant and disparate events as the Boston Tea Party, the Opium Wars, the siege of Hormuz and the seizure of St Helena. India was the greatest of its territories, the China trade the source of its fortunes, and the Mutiny the cause of its eventual demise.

By 1907, the role of the East India Company in India and the East had long been absorbed by the British Crown, and Edward VII was Emperor of an India which remained sufficiently strong and sure that in the darkest days of the Second World War serious consideration was given to relocating the seat of British power there. The legacy of the Company was not confined to the subcontinent, however, and dim echoes of its power can still be heard today – in China's reacquaintance with Hong Kong, in the rights of residency celebrations on St Helena, or in the clink of cocktail glasses in the Raffles Hotel in Singapore.

AN ELIZABETHAN INVENTION

On 31 December 1600, Elizabeth I put her signature to the Royal Charter which gave birth to the 'Governor and

William Moorcroft and his companion Hyder Hearsey in disguise meet two Tibetans near Lake Manasarowar, 1812.

Company of Merchants of London trading into the East Indies', commonly known as the East India Company. The concept had been gestating over many months in the City of London, but it required the Queen's authority to give form to the ambitions of the original subscribers, 218 merchants and tradesmen of the City.

The forces which gave rise to the Company, which was to become the largest and most prosperous that the world has ever seen, have been the subject of historical scrutiny ever since, and accounts vary according to historical predilections. However, without the particular circumstances of the Elizabethan age, they might have given rise to no more than a British version of those contemporary continental rivals which sprang up in the ensuing century – the 'Vereeinigde Oostindisches Compagnie' of Holland, the 'Compagnie des Indes' of France (founded 1664), and those of Denmark, Sweden and the Holy Roman Empire – all of which prospered and then faded whilst the East India Company eclipsed them all. Even today, we have no need to preface the name of the East India Company with 'British' or 'English'. It defined European adventurism in the East, and its successor, the British Empire, owed much of its power and prosperity to the foundations the Company had laid down.

Although the Queen died only two years after granting the Company its Charter, it was a supremely Elizabethan invention, the culmination of an age which saw England transformed from a second-rate, uncivilised, semi-piratical nation to a cultured, ambitious and revolutionary first-rank European power. The religious reformation instigated by Henry VIII and maintained by Elizabeth provided a secure, albeit renegade, identity which enabled the country to remain aloof from the depredations of the Thirty Years War (1618-48) which ravaged continental Europe; but it was the cultural context, with its unprecedented flowering of the dramatic arts and philosophy, which propelled the arrival of a new Golden Age, with Elizabeth as its Virgin Queen.

Marlowe's *Dr Faustus* contained at its core a paean to the limitless spiritual and temporal treasures that could be gained through heretical practices, and indeed the Company, disorganised and underfunded as it was, at times seemed impelled to a larger destiny as though by some mysterious force. Francis Yates attributes the concept of the British Empire to the Elizabethan magus, cartographer and philosopher John Dee. Influential at Court and versed in Hermetic thought, Dee had a mystical vision of a new

Jewels in the Crown

In 1607, the Third Voyage of the Company, commanded by William Keeling, arrived at the island of Socotra off the Horn of Africa – an unearthly place noted for its strange endemic plants. Here, amongst the bulbous cactii and aloes, the crew performed Shakespeare's Richard II, *with its moving patriotic verse:*

'This royal throne of kings, this scept'red isle,
This earth of majesty, this seat of Mars,
This other Eden, demi-paradise,
This fortress built by nature for herself
Against infection and the hand of war,
This happy breed of men, this little world,
This precious stone set in the silver sea . . .
This blessed plot, this earth, this realm,
this England . . .'

Against all reasonable expectations, the stage was set for this island race to rule over lands and seas in the East, and to acquire another, more exotic jewel – India itself.

European Golden Age with England in the lead; he could also boast a highly practical understanding of navigation, trade and commerce.

Edwin Jones calls the Reformation 'the greatest revolution in English history' (*The English Nation*, Sutton, 1998), which defined a prototypical nation statehood, aggressively nationalistic. England had previously played a minor part in a conservative, Catholic Europe. Now a new English pride linked to the Protestant faith gave the country a sense of destiny to fuel its expansionist ventures. The 'exclusive' trading rights asserted by the Spanish and Portuguese in the East were treated with as little respect by the defiant English as the Pope himself. The Dutch, though they had fought hard for their independence and the Protestant faith, and achieved an early advantage over the English in the East, failed to make the same lasting impact. They had to contend with their continental neighbours; the English were protected by the sea.

EARLY EUROPEAN VOYAGES
TO THE EAST

The eventual domination of European mercantile forces throughout most of the East, and the resultant Eurocentricism of the region's recent history, tends to exalt the early European explorers as though they 'discovered' much of the Indian Ocean and beyond. This conveniently ignores the existing regional trade, much of it conducted over astonishing distances in perilous circumstances. In ancient times, Herodutus reported that cinnamon came from African swamps guarded by bats, and was used by giant birds for their nests; scarcely more prosaically, significant trade certainly took place on the Cinnamon Route from Indonesia 4,000 miles across the Indian Ocean to Madagascar and as far north as Zanzibar, in double outrigger canoes. Likewise, the prodigious feats of the Grand Admiral Zheng He of China, the so-called 'Three Jewelled Eunuch', led to the appearance at Court in Peking in 1414 of a giraffe captured at Malindi in East Africa; the Chinese navy at that time dominated the Arabian Sea. (This was whilst the much-vaunted Henry the Navigator of Portugal was still struggling to get his ships down the coast of North West Africa.)

In Malindi, near where the giraffe was led on board an ocean-going junk, an unremarkable stone pillar, a *padrao*, can still be found, erected by Portuguese sailors to commemorate the place from which, a year earlier, they had set off across the Indian Ocean to become the first Europeans to sail all the way to India. That voyage irrevocably changed the history of the Indian Ocean, and with it, the East.

In 1498, the Portuguese fleet, led by the nobleman Vasco da Gama, reached Calicut, a rich trading city on the southwest coast of India. When asked why they had come, they replied, 'We seek Christians and spices,' portentously summarising that heady combination of trade and religion (or, as their detractors would argue, greed and bigotry) which was to colour the European presence in the East for the next century. Da Gama had been on a diplomatic, rather than an exploratory mission; he was supposed to make friendly relations with the rulers of the unknown East African coast

Queen Elizabeth I of England, whose signature on the Royal Charter gave birth to the East India Company.

beyond the Cape of Good Hope, which had been first rounded by his compatriot, Bartholomeu Dias, ten years earlier. Da Gama's idea of friendly relations was decidedly perverse – his sidekick, the curiously named Captain Major, tortured Muslim pilots with boiling pig fat for information to further their progress, and so alienated local rulers that one built a stockade to defend his water supplies. Da Gama's response was to blow up the stockade, then the nearest town for good measure. However, he did manage to ingratiate himself with the Sultan of Malindi, who recommended to him a Gujerati pilot, navigator and poet by the name of Ibn Majid, without whom Da Gama's small fleet would have been unable to make the crossing to Calicut. (Majid later lamented 'Oh! Had I known the consequences that would come from them! People were surprised by what they did!')

First to be surprised was the Zamorin, the local ruler in Calicut, who briefly held Da Gama and a number of his officers captive, before allowing them to purchase some spices and precious stones. Incensed by his imprisonment, Da Gama was not one to bear a grudge lightly, and on the voyage back mercilessly destroyed a naval force sent against him by the Zamorin's Goanese allies. When the next Portuguese fleet arrived in Calicut in 1500, under the command of Cabral, he ordered the Zamorin (being, according to Da Gama, a heretic Christian) to expel all Muslims from his realm and give the Portuguese precedence in trade. After a few weeks shilly-shallying, the inevitable calamity ensued, with fifty-three Portuguese slain in their trading compound, local merchants burnt alive, Calicut ravaged by cannon fire, and the Zamorin fled. Cabral then removed the dubious benefit of his custom to the neighbouring port of Cochin, whose rajah, no doubt fortified by the news from Calicut, sold him the spices he wanted at prices which would ensure that the 'curst Franks' would never lack for a financial motive in making the hazardous voyage around the Cape again.

In 1502, Da Gama himself led the fourth Portuguese fleet to Calicut in as many years, and remorselessly pursued his old enemy, committing atrocities against the Zamorin's subjects, the least of which was cutting the lips and ears off an emissary, sewing on the ears of dog, and sending him thus surgically enhanced back to the Zamorin. Amid blood, barbarity and bombardments, the spice race was born.

From their main base at Goa on the west coast of India the Portuguese sailed further east, establishing trading

*Sir Thomas Smyth, Founder Subscriber and First Governor of the
Company of Merchants of London trading to the East Indies.*

posts in Ceylon, Malacca and eventually at Macao, at the
mouth of the Pearl river near present-day Hong Kong, and
on the threshold of the mighty and unknown Chinese
Empire, where spices and silks could be obtained. Nutmeg
and cloves, two of the most valuable spices – mace, a third,
is derived from the outer skin of the nutmeg – came from
the Moluccas, known then as the Spice Islands, a tiny clus-
ter of islands east of Sulawesi. Forts were built there at
Ternate and Amboyna (now Ambon). By enforcing their
domination over rival Arab traders in the Indian Ocean
through superior naval firepower, and taking the strategic
port of Hormuz in the Persian Gulf, the Portuguese had
forged a chain from the source of spices back to Europe.
Their control of the spice trade was thus virtually complete,
and Lisbon was the spice capital of Europe.

By the remarkable Treaty of Tordesillas of 1494, Pope
Alexander VI had generously divided the unknown portions
of the planet between the rival interests of Spain and
Portugal by drawing a line of longitude a hundred leagues
west of the Azores, granting Spain everything west of it and
Portugal everything to the east. This arbitrary division led
to some far-reaching results; although at the time Spain
thought it had received the better deal, Portugal found itself
with the easiest passage to India, and, some years later, in
possession of Brazil. Like the East India Company's own
Charter, the treaty was not drafted with a fully rounded
global vision, and so it was that in 1543 Spanish galleons
could be found claiming the Philippines, having sailed west
across the Pacific from the New World. Despite being only
a few hundred miles from the Spice Islands, they avoided
outright conflict with their Portuguese rivals, but in the
ensuing years the position of both nations on the bridge of
naval power was under threat. The Spanish became
embroiled in a war over their possessions in the
Netherlands, which led to the creation of the independent
nation of Holland, and the united Spain and Portugal under
the Hapsburg Philip II was less formidable than the parts.

English seafarers such as Sir Francis Drake made full use
of their licence to plunder the hated Catholic Spanish ships,
and in a few years learnt as much about world navigation as
it had taken Spain and Portugal a hundred years to acquire.
They also found how vulnerable the enemy's bulky galleons
were to attack, and the overwhelming defeat by Drake of
the Spanish Armada (a defeat still seen in Spain as the result
of the intercession of dastardly English weather) ended the
myth of Iberian invincibility at sea. The capture in 1592 of
a Portuguese ship stuffed full of jewels, spices, porcelain,
silks and other luxuries from the East Indies caused a sen-
sation when it was unpacked at Dartmouth, as did the discovery on board of a register of the 'Government and Trade
of the Portuguese in the East Indies'. Both later reinforced
the Company's petition to the Queen for its Charter.

Both the English and the Dutch now turned their attention to the developing spice trade. The attempt to discover
a Northwest Passage to the East, via the Arctic Ocean, took
up time and effort, although it gave both nations a head start
in northeastern America. The hypothetical Northeast
Passage yielded no such compensations; the Dutch explorer
Willem Barents' discovery of his eponymous sea led to his
party being marooned all winter: ' . . . it was so extreme
cold, that the fire could almost cast no heate: for as we put

our feet to the fire, we burnt our hose before we could feel the heate, so that we had worke enough to doe to patch our hose: and which is more, if we had not sooner smelt, than felt them, we should have burnt them ere we had knowne it . . .' (Gerrit de Veer, 1596). Henry Hudson, partly funded by the East India Company, made a final fruitless attempt to find the Northwest Passage in 1610, and, like Barents, ended up with his name on the map, if only to mark his icy grave.

More success attended those who followed the traditional Portuguese route around the Cape of Good Hope. Captain James Lancaster, later to lead the First Voyage of the newly founded Company, found, in the style of Drake, that it was more productive to pillage from Portuguese vessels than actually to trade, but did make it as far as Penang, returning after an exhausting journey via the West Indies.

The Portuguese jealously guarded the secret of the sources of their spices, but information leaked out with the publication in Holland in 1596 of navigational maps, stolen by Jan van Linschoten from his employer, the Archbishop of Goa. The Dutch had not had the experience of the English of buccaneering around the Caribbean, and adopted an altogether more businesslike approach from the outset.

They sent a number of well-funded fleets to the Spice Islands in the late 1590s, seized Amboyna from the Portuguese, and effectively sealed off all possibility of direct trade in spices from the East India Company — which even then was being set up precisely to exploit that trade. By the time Linschoten's maps were translated, and the English had given up the lucrative pleasure of looting, it was too late for them to take up a more respectable trade.

THE COMPANY AND THE SPICE RACE

The First Voyage of the Company (each fleet, separately funded, was called a 'Voyage') set out in February 1601 under Captain James Lancaster. His flagship was the *Dragon*, the other vessels the *Hector*, the *Susan* and the *Ascension*. The fleet carried £28,472 of bullion for purchases, and goods worth a further £6,860, including wrought iron, crockery, pistols and spectacles. Lancaster knew enough about scurvy to take lemon juice aboard, but the captains of the other ships took the decision not to adopt this precaution. As a result, Lancaster's crew enjoyed full possession of their teeth all the way to the Cape, whilst many of the men in other ships parted company with theirs,

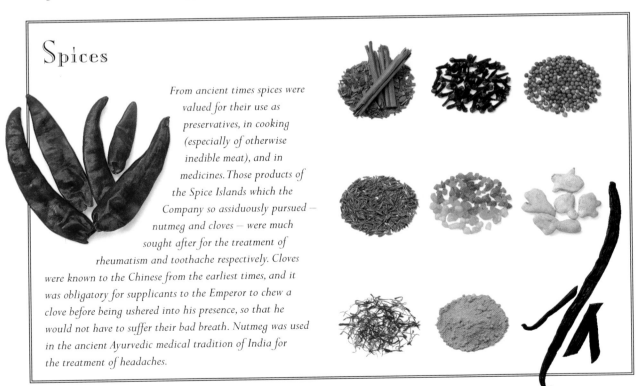

Spices

From ancient times spices were valued for their use as preservatives, in cooking (especially of otherwise inedible meat), and in medicines. Those products of the Spice Islands which the Company so assiduously pursued — nutmeg and cloves — were much sought after for the treatment of rheumatism and toothache respectively. Cloves were known to the Chinese from the earliest times, and it was obligatory for supplicants to the Emperor to chew a clove before being ushered into his presence, so that he would not have to suffer their bad breath. Nutmeg was used in the ancient Ayurvedic medical tradition of India for the treatment of headaches.

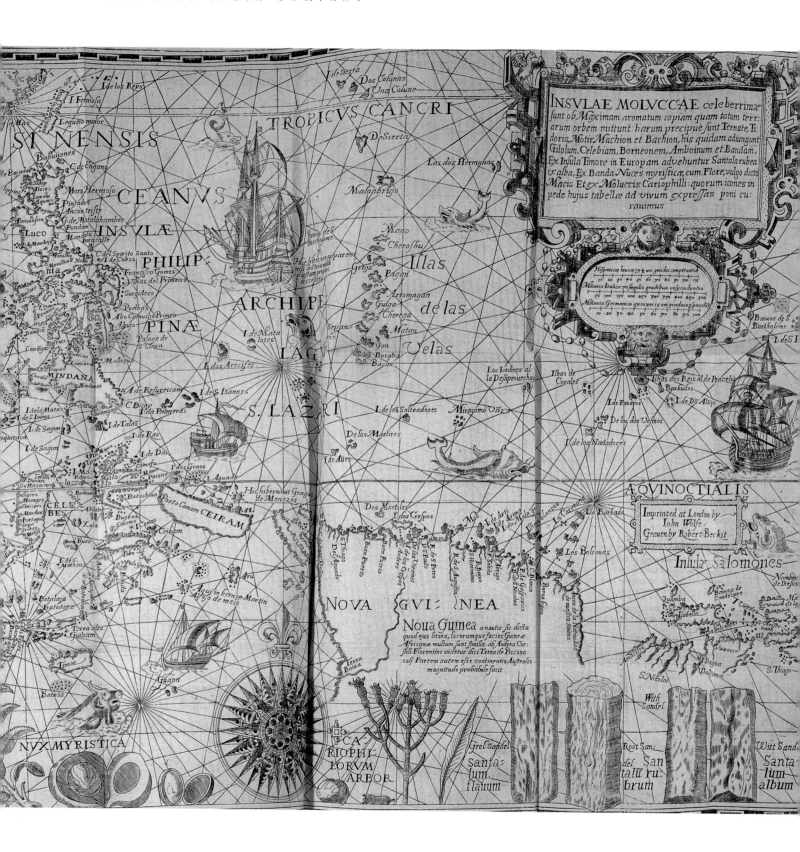

and 105 lost their lives altogether. (The use of lemon or lime juice, which seemed so clearly efficacious, surprisingly remained the matter of a captain's whim for years to come.)

After reprovisioning and recuperating at Table Bay, the fleet set sail again and arrived at Aceh in Sumatra in June 1602. Lancaster was amazed to find that the Sultan was keen to meet the English, having heard of their victory over the Spanish Armada. However, he quickly found that the Dutch had seized the initiative, and that to form trading alliances with the local potentates in the Spice Islands would be impossible without the substantial financial and military resources that the Dutch had provided for their fleets. The Dutch East India Company had raised a start up capital of £540,000 against the English Company's £68,373.

Thwarted in legitimate trade, Lancaster reverted to piracy, and managed to seize a large cargo of pepper and Indian cottons from a Portuguese ship. Inadvertently, he had stumbled upon what was to become a vital part of the Company's immediate trading future — the local Indian Ocean trade in 'piece' goods: cottons and printed textiles produced in South India, and sold in Java and Sumatra.

Lancaster was unable to purchase pepper at Aceh, but learnt that it was produced further down the coast. He also set up a trading 'factory' (a combination of fort and warehouse) at Bantam on Java, from which he could sell the purloined cottons. The Dutch were already trading from Bantam, but it was a major entrepôt for all the nations of the South China Sea and the presence of their arch rivals did not preclude good business. In fact, the Dutch proved positively eager to help when the factory was later attacked by Chinese arsonists and thieves, lending the English instru-

ments to torture a suspect; according to one of the Company's factors, 'between our men and the Flemmings, they shot him almost to pieces before they left him'. Such neighbourly consideration would not last long.

Having filled his holds with pepper, identified a source of further supplies, established a factory at Bantam, and learnt the value of the piece trade, Lancaster's command of the First Voyage of the East India Company could be judged a success. A reconnaissance mission to the Banda Islands (the nutmeg-producing part of the Moluccas) had admittedly turned up nothing more than belligerent Dutchmen, but after a hair-raising voyage back, he finally returned to England and a knighthood. There, the main disappointment was the pepper that he had brought back in high expectation of making a good profit. Unfortunately, James I had also captured a carrack full of pepper, so the London market was glutted and the price fell dramatically — as did the return for the investors, who had to make do with sacks of pepper instead of cash.

More seriously, thwarted by the Dutch, the First Voyage had failed to establish a direct trading link with the Spice Islands, and that failure was to dominate the Company's activities over the next twenty years.

Pepper, at least, was to remain one of the staples of the East India Company's spice trading right through to the nineteenth century, and the factories in Bantam in Java and later Bencoolen in Sumatra provided uninterrupted supplies. When the Company started to trade in South India and Ceylon, where cassia trees, the source of cinnamon, were indigenous, it was able finally to gain ready access to some of the spices that had thus far proved so elusive.

Linschoten's map of the Spice Islands which fuelled the spice race between the Dutch and the English Companies.

FIRST STEPS IN INDIA

'Thou by the Indian Ganges' side
Shouldst Rubies find: I by the tide
Of Humber would complain . . .'
Andrew Marvell 'To His Coy Mistress'

AMBASSADORS TO THE MOGHUL COURT

Thwarted in the Spice Islands, the Company quickly began to think of other ways of making the most of its Charter. It was known that there was substantial existing commerce between Surat in Gujerat, western India, all along the coast of the Arabian Sea to the Red Sea. In line with their new commercial strategy, on 31 December 1606 the Company's Court of Directors discussed the possibility of obtaining letters of introduction from James I to the then Turkish Governor of Aden, and the Third Voyage, under William Keeling, was ordered to call in on the region. Second in command was William Hawkins, who was valued for his fluent Turkish. After his ambitious staging of *Richard II* on Socotra (see page 11), Keeling left for Bantam, while Hawkins made for Surat in the indefatigable *Hector*.

Anchoring in a tidal creek downstream from the town, he quickly discovered the twin obstacles to trade: one, the corruption of the Moghul official in charge; the other, the Portuguese, 'who in troops lay lurking in the by-ways to give me assault to murther me'. Although Portugal was in theory at peace with England, the Portuguese scuttled any plans that the Company might have had by capturing two of the *Hector's* boats, along with their crews, and taking them off to Goa. The *Hector* then departed for Bantam, leaving Hawkins and his loyal sidekick William Finch to see what they could sell, and what trading rights they could obtain. Hawkins hired a bodyguard of Pathans, and, leaving Finch to look after their goods in Surat, headed off to Agra, ten weeks' journey away, to see the Moghul Emperor, Turkish-speaking Jehangir. He had become, de facto, the first English ambassador to the Moghul Court.

Hawkins impressed Jehangir with his Turkish and his seemingly unlimited capacity for drink, and, much to the chagrin of the Portuguese, became a firm favourite at Court. Jehangir found him an Armenian Christian wife, and gave him command of a troop of 400 cavalry, with the title of khan and a huge salary. He also promised vaguely to give the Company trading rights, which enabled Hawkins to accept the other perquisites as though part of a strategy to keep in Jehangir's favour for the Company's benefit.

His good fortune could not last; the Portuguese played on the jealousies among Jehangir's ministers, an English shipwreck disgorged a boatload of lustful, sottish sailors on Surat, and Jehangir grew tired of his company. He was dismissed, and left from Surat with his wife and entourage in tow, only to die on the voyage home. Hawkins had failed to extract firm trading concessions from Jehangir – the Emperor would in any case have seen no need to honour any such arrangement – but he had opened up the possibility of direct dealings between the Company and the Moghul Empire. His wife arrived in London a widow, badgered the Company for a pension, and finally married Gabriel Towerson, a senior Bantam factor, who founded the ill-fated Amboyna factory (see page 28).

In 1615, James I sent Sir Thomas Roe to the Court of Jehangir, on a mission to improve trade relations and extract the much sought-after trading privileges at Surat. The expedition was fully funded by the Company. Roe, in contrast to the sea-dog Hawkins, was an aristocratic career diplomat, with an endearing sense of his own 'qualitye' and an enduring contempt for that of anyone else. He refused to touch his head to the ground when meeting Jehangir's son, reporting, 'I came in honour to see the Prince, and was free from the custom of servants.' He was unimpressed by the Moghul Court at Agra when he got there – 'I never thought a Prince so famed would live so meanly' – and his self-important bearing seems to have impressed Jehangir. He may have been helped by the fact that in the three previous years the Company's small but agile fleets had managed to notch up a number of notable naval victories against Portuguese galleons sent from Goa against them. The bat-

The Indian Subcontinent, the playing field of the Company's territorial ambitions.

tles were a rerun in miniature of the Armada, and just as that victory had smoothed the Company's way with the Sultan of Aceh (see page 17), so these victories did not go unnoticed by Jehangir. The Portuguese had always relied on naval supremacy to enforce their control of shipping in the Arabian Sea, and their decline created a power vacuum; Indian vessels, whether full of merchandise or pilgrims to Mecca, needed protection from pirates, and if the Portuguese could no longer provide it, perhaps the Company could.

Roe left three years later, having achieved not the monopoly rights he sought, but a general permission to trade. This, given the machinations of the Portuguese, who were protective of their own increasingly fragile position, was more of an achievement than it seemed. Roe also advised the Company's Directors that 'War and trafique are incompatible', a suggestion which the Company implemented with a resounding lack of success over the next two hundred and fifty years.

COFFEE FROM MOCHA

The East India Company, like the English themselves, has an indelible association with tea. However, at the start of the seventeenth century the Company was more concerned with coffee, and by the end the century coffee was being consumed in England far more widely than tea. Only after 1750 did the Company, and the country, become thoroughly immersed in tea.

The Company had many directors and shareholders in common with the Levant Company, incorporated in 1579, and had thereby received intelligence about the potential commercial significance of coffee – as yet unknown in Europe. They were aware from maps and information provided by Richard Hakluyt (the cartographer whom the Company had, with a sense of destiny, appointed historiographer in 1603) that it could only be obtained from the Turkish port of Mocha, at the southern end of the Red Sea in Arabia Felix (now Yemen). Keeling had failed to make useful contacts there, but while Hawkins was carousing with Jehangir, the *Ascension* had called at Mocha with John Jourdain aboard. After travelling through the mountains with their coffee plantations, he recorded his appraisals of the cultivation and drinking of coffee, and the observation that 'coffee is a great merchandise for it is carried to Grand Cairo and all other places of Turkey and the Indies'. He

Europeans at Moghul Court. Probably Portuguese, they appear to be drinking coffee, then popular at the Court.

obtained permission from the Pasha at Sana'a, the capital, to trade from Mocha, and the Directors diverted the three ships of the next Voyage to Mocha, in expectation of establishing trade between there and Surat, where Hawkins was thought to be on the verge of obtaining concessions.

At first all went well. The fleet under the command of Sir Henry Middleton included the new *Trades' Increase* (see

Sir Thomas Roe

Roe came equipped with all the lineaments of a diplomat. Tall, moustachioed and goatee'd, he had an unswerving sense of protocol. He took no pleasure in nautch dances or drinking parties, was constantly short of cash and too proud to ask for help, and was only interested in 'free and peaceable trade with the English'. In short, a perfect ambassador for King and Company, but not much fun. For all his urbanity, he was as ignorant of the geography of the East as most: 'Here are none of the rarities of India; they all come from the Eastern part [i.e. China]'.

As befitted his station, he had a chaplain, a surgeon and the standard ambassador's trunk, used from Elizabeth I's time onwards. About three feet high over its domed top and about five feet long, it was covered with leather, studded with brass, and decorated with the Royal Coat of Arms. It contained porcelain and silver for entertaining formally in the stead of the Sovereign; whether Roe had the opportunity to deploy it is not recorded. He also had worthy presents to offer — Jehangir took particular delight in his present of a coach, complete with English coachman.

Roe's opinion of Moghul India was decidedly unfavourable: 'Religions infinite; laws none. In that confusion what can be expected?' He observed closely the famous annual weighing of the Emperor against his wealth in gold and precious stones, and finally silver, which was distributed among the poor, 'but I saw none, it being in bagges it might bee pebbles . . . I saw it carefully carryed in, and none distributed'.

page 67) and *Peppercorn,* and arrived at Mocha in October 1609. The English appeared to be made welcome by the local Turkish official, but suddenly the situation turned hostile. Their house was besieged, eight crew members were killed, and Middleton was held prisoner. Refusing to order his fleet to surrender, he was transported, clapped in irons, to Sana'a. He learnt from the Pasha that the Mocha merchants were concerned about the English buying up all the Indian goods and strangling their trade; Middleton promised that they would not do so, whereupon he was taken back to Mocha, still a captive. When he finally escaped, in a water butt, he made off with his fleet for Surat but later returned to Mocha to wreak his revenge by confiscating the goods of fifteen Gujerati trading ships waiting to enter port. This may have satisfied Middleton, but it ruined the Company's reputation in Surat and undermined negotiations already underway with a new official there. Far from finding a way to participate in local trade, the Company had managed to alienate those who might have helped them. It took the negotiating skills of Sir Thomas Roe to re-establish good relations. As he smoothed ruffled feathers, he observed the consumption of coffee at the Moghul Court. Roe might be the subject of the picture opposite, which shows a European drinking coffee there.

Coffee, the 'Wine of Araby'. The Company became involved in the coffee trade out of Mocha before it had been seen in Europe.

21

Thanks to Roe, the Company was soon engaged in the coffee trade in earnest. William Finch, Hawkins' loyal number two, fetched up as agent in Mocha in 1619, and was soon busy sending consignments of coffee to colleagues in Surat in preference to those in Persia, as it 'was worth more in Surat than your advice valued it there'. William Burt wrote to the Company from Isfahan in 1630 that 'if ships go to Mocha with a well-chosen cargo they will do well, especially if invested in cowa (coffee) seeds, which find vent both in Surat and Persia unto your large advantage'.

Early in the eighteenth century, the enterprising Dutch took coffee plants from Arabia to their possessions in the East Indies, establishing substantial coffee plantations there. The East India Company, however, was slow to cultivate coffee in their possessions; in 1732 there are records of the Company taking seeds to cultivate on St Helena, but it was not until the nineteenth century that it developed the first commercial plantations in India and Ceylon. By the end of that century, coffee had become a hugely popular international commodity, and although the French and the Dutch had been far more instrumental in the spread of its cultivation, the East India Company was the first western company to be directly involved in the coffee trade.

THE PIECE TRADE

The 'piece trade' referred to the Company's trade in the bewildering variety of textiles from India. To the familiar litany of calicoes, muslins, dungarees, ginghams, bandanas,

A Moghul tent hanging; even on the move, standards were lavishly maintained.

A silk embroidered bodice made in India for the British market as part of the 'piece trade'.

cambrics, chintzes, seersuckers and taffetas should be added the less celebrated alliballies, humhums, jamdanies, nainsooks, sassergates and many more. Relating the names to the textiles, sorting out the often tiny differences between them, and coping with the overlaps and regional variations, was one of the most arduous tasks facing a Company factor; not surprisingly, confusion often crept into correspondence and official reports.

Lancaster's capture at Aceh of the Portuguese ship containing Indian cloths had shown that it was possible to make money from the local Indian Ocean textile trade, and the Company applied itself to establishing factories in the main textile-producing areas of India – first at Surat, which they reached in 1608, then at Masulipatam on the Coromandel coast, reached in 1611, and later in Bengal. They soon found that the quality of the cloth they were able to buy was not

A palampore (bedcover) of painted and dyed cotton. From the Coromandel coast, late 18th century.

only suitable for trade in Java and Sumatra, but could find a ready market at home. The piece trade was not the spice trade, but at least it was merchandise which could justify the risk and expense of the Company's Voyages. Without this piece trade, the Company would have faced disaster in the early years; whilst the Company's long-held dream of exporting fine woollen English broadcloth to the East was never realised, it was as cloth merchants that they survived.

Surat traded mainly dyed calicoes (cotton), carpets and 'Guinea cloths', a blue check cloth which was popular in West Africa and the West Indies. The Coromandel produced fine chintzes, a sophisticated four-stage dyed cotton cloth, and Bengal was the home of muslins and silks. The importance of the piece trade can be judged by the fact that in each of these three areas the Company later founded its own trading factory; these – Bombay, Madras and Calcutta – became the Company's 'Presidencies' (see chapter 5), and have since developed into the largest cites of modern India.

Chintzes were ideal as furnishing fabrics, as they retained their strong colours, and were also sufficiently cheap to be affordable by the emerging middle classes in England. By the late seventeenth century they were much in vogue for rooms with an Indian theme; the English were fascinated by the tales they heard of the East Indies from the Company's activities, and the fabric was a tangible expression of those exotic ideas. They were noted for a vibrant red colour produced by a dye found only in the north Coromandel, which became known as 'East India madder'. Indigo, the blue vegetable dye which required no 'mordant' (fixer), was the other classic Indian dye used in chintzes and other textiles, and its cultivation and trade remained commercially important throughout the Company's time.

As the piece trade matured, so the manufacturers of the cloths began to respond to their new European patrons, and particular themes were incorporated at their request, the most usual being Coats of Arms, which found their way onto wallhangings, bedcovers and carpets.

The Fremlin Carpet, made for the Company's President of Council in Surat in 1637.

THE SPICE ISLANDS AND JAPAN

> '... out of the abundance of ffruit which some region enjoyeth, the necessitie or wante of others should be supplied'.
>
> Letter of Introduction from Elizabeth I to Eastern rulers

CLASHES WITH THE DUTCH

The Dutch East India Company, though it tolerated the Company's presence on its fringes, had no intention of giving any ground in the Spice Islands themselves. The Dutch had already seized the Portuguese forts at Amboyna and Ternate, and had used their muscle to intimidate local rulers into exclusive trading treaties which kept the English at bay. This was made easier by the fact that the Company rarely had more than one ship available for exploratory trading missions in the islands, and usually had to rely on evading the Dutch to obtain any sort of cargo. Spice-running, rather than spice trading, was the order of the day. Political negotiations back home to secure the freedom to trade were interminable and likely to be ignored. In 1614, Jan Pieterson Coen wrote from Batavia (Djakarta) to his masters in Amsterdam, 'Your honours should know by experience that trade in Asia must be driven and maintained under the protection and favour of Your Hounours' own weapons . . . we cannot carry on trade without war nor war without trade.' This fiercely pragmatic attitude is in startling contrast to Roe's considered view.

The Company was able to seize one nutmeg of consolation from the Dutch. Pulo Run is a minuscule volcanic island on the edge of a tiny group of islands called the Banda Islands, themselves the only nutmeg-producing portion of the Spice Islands. It fell into Company hands in 1616, and although its nutmeg crop was small, the island assumed

Map of the East Indies and the Spice Islands, held at the British Library. Late 16th century.

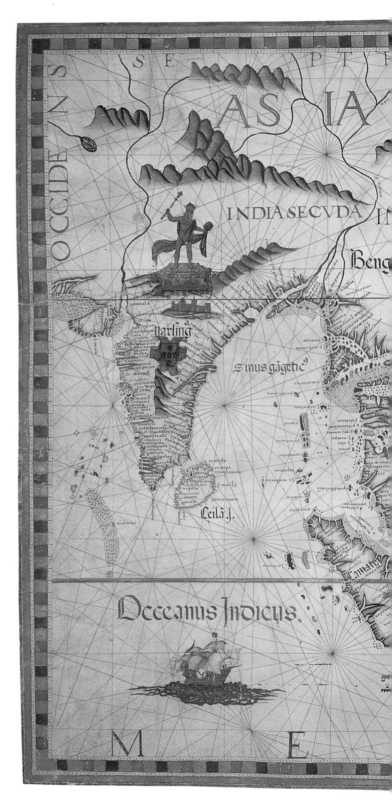

great significance as the one Company enclave amid the all-powerful Dutch. The local inhabitants swore allegiance to King James, and such was the attachment felt by the British for this musket-shot wide outpost of Empire that James I even styled himself 'King of England, Scotland, Ireland and Pulo Run'.

Run had not escaped the attention of the vigilant Dutch and the Company had to survive a surreal siege to secure it: Nathaniel Courthorpe took possession of the island in October 1616, with two ships, both of which were quickly captured by the Dutch. Refusing to negotiate a surrender despite constant harassment, Courthorpe repeatedly sent native boats with pleas for help to his countrymen in Bantam. When two ships eventually came to attempt a rescue in 1618, they too were captured by a Dutch fleet which arrived at precisely the wrong moment. Then a war of attrition broke out between the rival Companies in the whole East Indies, undermining any hopes that Courthorpe may have harboured of relief. Down to thirty-eight men and minimum rations, things were looking grim, especially as he had to beg sustenance from the islanders in return for the Company's protection, which, after four years, must have seemed chimerical. He escaped from a Dutch ship which had captured him and his men as they rowed to a neighbouring island, but drowned just in time to miss the news of the 1619 treaty, which was supposed to reconcile the Companies' trading interests in the Spice Islands. It did no such thing, of course, and soon the Dutch had overrun Run, and as fast as the Company set up factories at Amboyna, Ternate and the Bandas, they made plans to abandon them. In the event, the Dutch saved them the trouble and expense of removing themselves from Amboyna; in 1623, they captured and tortured horribly the fifteen Englishmen there, including Gabriel Towerson, the factor from Bantam whose widow-to-be had already been widowed once by Hawkins (see page 18). They were executed in spite of their being no proof of the charges of spying that were laid against them, and when the news of the 'Amboyna Massacre' eventually reached England a year later there was talk of war and bloody reprisals – which came to nothing more than Dryden's epic poem 'Amboyna'. The Company had by ruthless force been prised from the Spice Islands, and soon lost its toehold in Batavia as well, leaving only the factories at Macassar and Bantam to dabble diligently in trade.

And what of Pulo Run? Never officially lost, it was a constant pawn in peace negotiations between the Dutch and the

English, and was eventually handed back to the Crown in 1665. In the meantime, the Company had come up with a plan to colonise the island, and had assembled twenty-seven English settlers who were willing to seek a new life for themselves in the unknown East. It was probably just as well that it was unknown, as at the last minute the party was diverted to the Company's newly acquired island of St Helena (see pages 79–81) in the South Atlantic. Instead of being wafted by spicy breezes under the nutmeg trees of Run, the settlers were to be blasted by the south-east trades on an island a mere 10,000 miles as the albatross flies from their supposed destination.

Never more than a bastion of English pride, Pulo Run was eventually ceded to the Dutch under the Treaty of

Breda in 1667, in return for a small island off the American seaboard called New Amsterdam. The Dutch thought they had got the better of the deal at the time, but the inhabitants of present-day Manhattan might disagree.

FIRST APPROACHES TO JAPAN

Although the East India Company had been set up primarily as an importing company, in contrast to the export-led activities of the Levant Company, and two other chartered trading companies of the time, the Muscovy and Eastland companies, the Directors were mindful that the constant drain on bullion reserves resulting from their trade was politically unpopular. Ideally, they would have liked to sell

The return of the Dutch East India Company fleet to Amsterdam, more impressive by far than its English rival.

English woollen broadcloth to a third party in exchange for bullion, and then use that bullion to buy the spices which were the main target of their early trade. Recognising that the inhabitants of the tropical East Indies were unlikely to show much interest in their woollens, they looked north to the virtually unknown lands of Japan and China.

John Saris, a thirty-two-year-old factor at the Company's factory at Bantam in Java, submitted a report to the Directors in 1608, in which he suggested that Japan represented a fine commercial opportunity. His view was confirmed shortly afterwards in letters from William

Adams, an Englishman who had been acting as pilot for a Dutch fleet, and had settled in Japan from 1600. There he had built a remarkable career for himself as principal marine architect to the shogun, had taken a Japanese wife – whilst still finding time to write to his English wife and family – and was prepared to lend his assistance to his countrymen in establishing trade. Japan was, he wrote, 'an Indies of money' and 'there is here much silver and gold [which would] serve their turnes in other places'. In addition, Adams felt that Japan would provide a good market for broadcloth.

This was exactly what the Court of Directors wished to hear. Armed with copies of Linschoten's charts, Saris was commissioned to take a ship from the Eighth Voyage, the *Clove*, and proceed from Bantam on a reconnaissance mission to Japan, with the aim of establishing a factory. When he finally arrived in Hirado (a small island off the west coast

of Kyushu) in 1613, he was warmly received – too warmly, perhaps, as he had great difficulty in keeping his crew from the whorehouses. He himself staged private viewings of his collection of pornographic paintings for the local women-folk, though he was astonished when they bowed down before one image that they took to be the Virgin Mary (many locals having been converted by the Jesuits). Pleasures there were many, but business was more difficult. William Adams, when he finally surfaced, was a disappointment; he seemed scarcely pleased to see his countrymen, and gave a gloomy prognosis for the Company's trading prospects.

It was first necessary to obtain permission from the shogun to set up a factory. Adams accompanied Saris to Yedo (Tokyo), and a remarkable account of their trip survives, describing the size and splendours of the cites of Fukuoke, Osaka, Shizuoka (Sampu) and Yedo. Amazed by the sophis-

East Asia, showing the extent of the Company's real or attempted trading interests.

tication of the roads, the people, the cities and the temples, Saris' letters were greeted with profound scepticism back in England, 'The loudest lies I have ever seen,' pronounced King James, with more than a hint of chauvinism.

It was shortly after this, in 1615, that the use of the word for tea is first recorded in English. A Company factor, Mr Wickham, writing to his friend Mr Eaton in Hirado, asks him to buy a 'pot of the best sort of chaw in Meaco', the place where the tea was grown for the shogun. There is further evidence from letters between other Englishmen that tea-drinking was well established amongst them, some fifty years before Catherine of Braganza's marriage to Charles II led to its popularity in England (see page 40).

Saris left in the *Clove* in 1613, leaving Adams and 'honest Mr Cocks' in charge. His return to England the following September was by no means a triumph. To the fury of the Directors waiting for the vessel in London, he first put in at Plymouth, where he unloaded his private trade. A letter from Saris to his brother, asking him to meet him with a barge at Gravesend, was intercepted and confirmed the Directors' suspicions that he was attempting to evade their scrutiny. When Saris finally arrived in London, he was dismissed, and a bonfire made of his pornographic books and paintings in the courtyard of the Company's headquarters.

Trade in woollen broadcloth to the Japanese was not a success, perhaps in part attributable to the fact that the Company factors themselves wore fine silks, while their sailors wore crude fustian. The Japanese were thus understandably slow to appreciate the merits of the broadcloth which the merchants seemed unwilling to wear themselves.

What with the intense rivalry of the Dutch, the unhelpfulness of the taciturn Adams, and the suspicious letters he received from his superiors in Bantam, even honest Mr Cocks took time out from his gardening – he introduced the potato to Japan – to rail against his unenviable situation in Hirado. Ships were few and far between, trade was at a standstill, and he had to withdraw his factors from Yedo and Osaka. By early 1620, the Dutch had put a price on his head and fought pitched battles outside the English factory. A ship bought news of a temporary respite in the shape of the Anglo-Dutch agreement in late 1620, and for a while, much to the astonishment of their Japanese hosts, the rivals became firm friends, thriving on the looting of silks from Chinese junks trading across to Manila from the South China coast. At last the English factory prospered, but when Adams died, and the alliance fell apart, Bantam decided to retrench.

A ship brought orders to close the remains of the factory in Hirado; Mr Cocks had to leave his fine collection of goldfish, and some of his colleagues had to abandon bemused wives and families as the Company finally pulled out in 1623.

Thereafter, despite their formidable successes in opening up the trade with China, Siam, Cochin and Burma (see chapter 4), the East India Company had little direct contact with Japan. In 1673, they endeavoured to reopen a factory – in

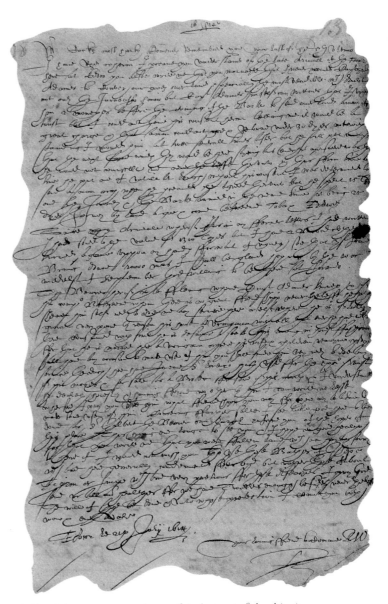

Wickham's letter, mentioning 'a pot of the best sort of chaw' (tea), written in the undecipherable script characteristic of the time.

Catharina D:G: Mag: Brit: Fra: et Hib: Regina
Filia Joannis IIII Reg: Portug: &c.

I. Haysmans pinx: I. Smith fec:

Export goods from Japan

Japan, despite its apparent reluctance to admit foreigners, nevertheless made exceptional goods for the export market. The lacquer chest (below) was ordered for the Duke of Devonshire at Chatsworth, one of four such chests ordered by the Dutch East India Company, which was endearingly unspecific about decoration, demanding only that they be 'finely and extraordinarily' made. The Dutch company bought a number of large-scale items such as these, including two palanquins intended as a present to the Moghul Emperor.

The writing slope (left) was likewise an export product, and it is interesting to note that although its shape is western, its decoration remains resolutely Japanese in contrast to the Regency-style slopes manufactured later in China.

competition, as always, with the Dutch. The Japanese authorities had earlier expelled the Jesuits and their Portuguese patrons, who had been causing a great deal of trouble. When the English reappeared, the Dutch informed the authorities that the English were in alliance with the Portuguese (which was not true), and that Charles II had taken a Portuguese wife (which was). Japan refused to entertain the opening of an English factory. It was not until the founding of Hong Kong (see page 177) that the Company came into regular contact with the Japanese again.

English attempts to make headway in Japan may appear to have ended ignominiously, but the Portuguese had been expelled in 1639, and although the Dutch continued to be the sole western trading presence, from 1641 until the 1850s this was from the relative backwater of Deshima in Nagasaki harbour.

Catherine of Braganza, the Portuguese bride of Charles II of England, who converted the Court to tea-drinking.

THE COMPANY IN CHINA

'What did it export from England? Courage. And what did it import from China? Tea.'
C N Parkinson, *Trade in the Eastern Seas*, 1937

FIRST CONTACT

China had been known as a source of various exotic and luxurious goods since ancient times, and the East India Company was keen to start trading there. The Company's first ship to visit, the *London,* in 1637, was followed by Commander John Weddell's attempts, on behalf of the rival Courteen Association, to open up commercial contacts in 1637; neither visit was attended with great success. The Manchu Emperor eventually opened his ports to foreign trade in 1685, and the Company's first trading post was at Amoy, although with the rapid rise of the tea trade in the late seventeenth century, Canton became better placed to service their requirements.

THE CANTON FACTORIES

Canton, a port on the Pearl river upstream from Hong Kong and Macao, had been the natural entrepôt for China and other eastern nations long before the Europeans arrived; Arab traders had been established there since the Tang dynasty (618-906 AD). Although the manufacture of ceramics and silks took place hundreds of miles away, the desire of the Chinese emperors to keep their nation closed to foreigners (whilst at the same time profiting from their trade) led to the rise of a sophisticated internal trading network, with only the merchants of Canton and other Chinese ports exposed to scrutiny by outsiders. It was this well-established network that first the Portuguese and then other European nations tapped into. After 1729, all foreign trade was restricted to Canton.

The Emperor maintained strict direct control of the Canton trade through an imperial agent and the 'Co-Hong' system of licensed Chinese merchants. Western trading nations were allowed to establish factories along the Canton waterfront: the East India Companies of Holland, England, Sweden, France, Denmark and the Holy Roman Empire were later joined by merchants from the United States. Initially, trade was dominated by the Dutch and English East India Companies, but by 1730, the English had supremacy. Their palatial waterfront factory had a lush mature garden which was the envy of other nations, and a balcony from which to survey it. The factory typically housed 12 Supercargoes (officers in charge of commercial activities), eight writers (clerks), two tea inspectors, two surgeons and a chaplain. A road named Hog Lane passed along the back of all the factories, renowned for its thieves and prostitutes.

Yet, despite their well-established air, the factories only operated seasonally, when the winds of the South China Sea allowed. In the winter months they were empty, and the merchants all moved down to Macao to wait at leisure for the next season, occupying themselves with balls, cricket matches and the social round.

Life for a Company servant in Canton was potentially very lucrative. A posting in the lowly rank of writer was usually acquired by patronage, and one of the most jealously guarded privileges of the Directors of the Company was their influence over the selection process, enabling them to place relatives and friends in positions that could make their fortunes. A writer would be paid £100 a year, but that might rise in five years to £1,000, with all living expenses paid. The Supercargoes, permanently based in China, could, with commissions, earn £9,000 a year, which was enough for a comfortable retirement after a few years' service. Nor was the work too exacting, as business was sporadic and the Chinese, for all their reputation, pleasant to deal with – the Hongs took back substandard tea without demur, and even trusted merchants to dump such tea in London to avoid having to bring it all the way back to Canton to be credited.

Chinese artists recorded views of the Canton waterfront for their European patrons. The early oil on canvas painting by Sunqua (over) shows the relatively disorganised state of the area in front of the European factories. European artists also recorded the oriental scene, and Chinese artists were commissioned to work in the European style. One of only

Early 19th-century Chinese painted wallpaper for export evolved from the plain wallpaper used in local houses.

The Canton waterfront by Sunqua, showing the European factories; the Company's garden and balcony were the envy of others.

two 'face-makers', or portrait sculptors, working in Canton was Amoy Chinqua, to whom this portrait of a European gentleman is attributed. The figure has not been identified, but seems likely to have been a merchant in the service of the Danish East India Company.

PORCELAIN

For artistic and technical reasons, much is made of the discovery and importation of porcelain from China, yet for most of the eighteenth century it rarely formed more than two per cent of the total annual value of the Company's China trade, and by the end of the century had dwindled to next to nothing as home manufacturers such as Josiah Wedgwood competed successfully with the imports.

In artistic terms, there were broadly speaking three phases in the porcelain trade between the East India Company and China. Until around 1700, Chinese crafts-men adapted to western demand to the extent that they made specific shapes for the European market, but retained traditional Chinese decorations. Most popular were designs in blue and white, kraak and rolwagen ware. The second phase saw China effectively competing with European manufacturers to create goods to an entirely western specification, including more highly coloured designs known as Imari ware, and figurines. The third phase, from the late eighteenth century, saw a re-emergence of the demand for Chinese designs – a fashion that came to be known as Chinoiserie. This is sometimes seen as a return to tradi-

Amoy Chinqua's portrait of a Danish merchant in Canton. Mid-18th century.

A Man-of-War at anchor with a Chinese junk beyond, off an unidentified tropical coast, c.1838.

tional Chinese decoration, but in truth it was a romanticised western idea of earlier designs, and much debased. The famous 'willow pattern' design beloved of the western market is an example of this; the so-called 'rice grain' pattern (leading to transparent patterns on the porcelain), on the other hand, had deeply traditional roots.

Some porcelain was commissioned to mark specific events – in the case of the Haeslingfield shipwreck, to mark a fortunate survival. The commemorative bowls (over) were probably commissioned by the Indiaman's comman-

der, Robert Haldane, and given to the crew which survived a hurricane en route to Canton. Each bowl was inscribed with a crew member's name, and each picture hand-drawn by James Beech, an amateur artist who was also a survivor of the wreck.

Chinese porcelain figurines of humans and animals were used only in rituals and in tombs; it was western influence which gave rise to their ornamental uses. One of the earliest examples shows a pair of King Charles spaniels – a breed which was introduced to the West from eastern Asia – and may have been a gift to King Charles from the East India Company. These were coloured, but another small export trade existed in the much-admired plain white porcelain figurines from Dehua known as *blanc de chine*. A porcelain cup with a moulded plum blossom decoration in the same material was frequently copied in the West.

The Chinese porcelain industry was concentrated around Jingdezhen in southern central China, but after 1729 all trade contacts with Europeans were restricted to Canton, and within fifty years English domestic manufacturers were supplying most of the demand. By the 1800s as few as 5,000 items of Chinese porcelain found their way to England a year.

Chinese porcelain was initially popular with western customers who had some involvement in the East India Company; later, most of the great families of Europe had ordered whole dinner services emblazoned with their own Coats of Arms. By the nineteenth century, services such as these could be bought in Europe, and in 1805 the Company itself ordered an armorial dinner service for an Indian Presidency from Worcester, rather than Canton. By this time, the main items coming from China were single extraordinary pieces such as the grand Mandarin vases familiar in country houses of that era and exotica such as highly decorated nine-foot tall pagodas. The 'ginger jar', a porcelain container for the storage of root ginger, became the most popular ordinary item of porcelain for the home market, and ginger itself became an indispensable ingredient in cookery.

Sample patterns on Chinese porcelain designed to show to potential customers in England.

A porcelain dinner service bearing the arms of the Company intended for the Madras Presidency, recovered from a wreck off Malacca.

By far and away the single most important trading commodity for the East India Company from China was tea, and that gave rise to an interesting design development. The Chinese were used to brewing tea in powdered form in teacups, but towards the end of the fourteenth century larger-leafed teas had become popular, and these required a brewing vessel. The Chinese had adapted their traditional wine pots to this purpose, adding a handle and a spout, and the English latched onto this design when they became interested in tea; many stoneware pots of this kind were exported back to England. This in turn spawned its imitators, principally in Staffordshire, and the familiar 'Brown Betty' teapot evolved.

The survivors of the wreck of the Haeslingfield were presented with a commemorative punch bowl in 1744.

TEA

Tea was not the initial target of the Company's trade with China, but it rapidly assumed enormous significance, and from the mid-eighteenth century onwards was by far and away the most important item of trade. Tea had been used in ancient China for many thousands of years, and also, probably, in Burma and Siam – at first for medicinal purposes, but later as a beverage. In the twelfth century, the Japanese learnt about the cultivation and drinking of tea from their neighbour, China, while Russia was the first European nation to import tea on camel trains across the Gobi desert – the tea was compressed into bricks for easy transportation, and the round trip from China took three years. Some tea reached England via the private trade of the Company's servants – the 'China drink' was mentioned in 1658 in an advertisement for the Sultaness Head Copheehouse in the City. However, it was a king's marriage which put tea on the map.

When, in the sixteenth century, the Portuguese established their trading post at Macao at the mouth of the Pearl river, they adopted the local custom of drinking tea. In 1662, Charles II of England married the Portuguese princess Catherine of Braganza, and she probably introduced the English Court to the pleasures of tea, although the Company's minute book records a gift of tea to the King in 1664. In either case, with royal patronage assured, within a short time it had become hugely popular. The Company was ideally placed to make money from the new fashion, and by 1687 was confidently placing an order via Bombay to Amoy for 20,000 pounds of tea 'extraordinarily good, being for England'. By 1750, it was shipping over two and a half million pounds of tea a year, and this could comfortably fetch five shillings a pound at auction in London – at least twice the cost price in Canton. Swingeing duties, sky-high prices, smuggling and adulteration all failed to dent the ever-rising popularity of tea; by 1800 imports had reached over twenty million pounds a year, producing more revenue than the whole of India. The humble leaf of *Camellia Sinensis* was more commercially important to the Company than all the pomp and circumstance of the Company raj.

The teas exported from China to Europe and America in the seventeenth and at the beginning of the eighteenth century were predominantly green (unfermented) teas, and were called by curious names, most of which have now disappeared – Hyson Skin, Bing, Caper, and Twankey (after which Gilbert and Sullivan's Widow Twankey was named). Black Souchong and Congou teas became increasingly popular in England, as well as the most expensive, Pekoes. One tea was not exported and was reserved for the Emperor and his Court. This came from wild tea bushes in Yunnan province, which grew to such a height that the tips could only be plucked by specially trained monkeys. About two hundred pounds of this 'Imperial Monkey-Picked Tea' was produced each season.

THE MACARTNEY MISSION AND EARL GREY TEA

In 1793, Lord Macartney led a mission to Peking and the Chinese Emperor's summer palace at Jehol. The mission's aims were laudable – the removal of trading handicaps at Canton; the regulation of the Hongs, who had a propensity to default on unsecured loans; and the administration of Chinese justice – but although it was funded by the Company to the tune of £80,000, the Directors were rightly sceptical that anything of lasting value would be achieved. Macartney was a career diplomat with connections at the highest level, but he had already run foul of Warren Hastings as a result of his high-handed behaviour and distinct lack of diplomatic instinct when he was made Governor of Madras in 1781. He refused to recognise Hastings' authority, interfered with Sir Eyre Coote's prosecution of the war against Hyder Ali – even offering him a peace settlement without Hastings' knowledge – and made various other gaffes. This behaviour, however, in those volatile times, was nothing out of the ordinary. The mission was conducted in considerable style – his entourage was ninety-five strong, including five German musicians – but his refusal to kow-tow to the Emperor (which gave rise to the popular expression) and the gifts he brought both failed to impress.

The Macartney Mission may have failed to achieve its aims, but it did give an opportunity for its participants to study China more closely than any westerners before. It included an artist, William Alexander, charged with recording the scene, and, in Sir George Staunton, an eminent botanist who was also secretary to Macartney. Staunton may well have played a role in the development of the blend of tea scented with bergamot which we now know as Earl Grey. Sir Joseph Banks – the founder of modern economic botany who was also an advisor to the Company – was inter-

A tea packing factory in Canton, showing a European merchant discussing business.

ested in the potential for growing tea in India. Before the Macartney Mission left for Peking, he briefed Staunton to observe carefully and record the Chinese methods of cultivating and scenting tea. As an example of how he would like the botanical drawings to be executed, he showed Staunton an illustration of the bergamot orange (*Citrus Bergamia*).

Staunton's report on his findings in China, edited by Banks in 1796, contained some general observations on flavouring processes, and mentioned the cultivation of tea shrubs among orange bushes (the Chinese bitter orange, *Citrus Aurantium*). Banks, an inveterate experimenter with exotic foods since his days with Captain Cook, had a tea-

house in the basement of his house in Soho Square. With his librarian and factotum Doctor Solander, later to be known for his 'Sanitive Tea', Banks experimented with many different tea flavourings along the lines suggested by Staunton, and almost certainly tried the addition of the commonly available bergamot oil, as being the nearest thing to the Chinese bitter orange. The recipe for Earl Grey tea most likely resulted.

The recipe was named after the prime minister Earl Grey, who was popular among the newly enfranchised and wealthy urban bourgeoisie – precisely those most likely to favour a new blend of tea. The myth that he discovered the

41

recipe in China is still widely promulgated, despite there being no evidence that he ever went there, and the fact that bergamot is strictly a European subspecies.

Lord Macartney was the principal beneficiary of his mission, returning as he did to England and an Earldom. He was notably more successful than William, 1st Earl Amherst, who slogged his way with seventy-five men to China in 1816 as 'Ambassador Extraordinary to the Emperor'. On arrival in Peking, he was immediately ordered into the imperial presence, but declined, pleading exhaustion. The Emperor, incensed at his presumption, ordered him to leave Peking without an audience. Amherst weathered this blow to his career admirably, becoming Governor General in India, invading Burma, and establishing Simla as a fashionable resort.

TEA AND FREE TRADE

The commercial success of the Company's monopoly on trade in tea attracted understandable envy, and fuelled the Free Trade movement at Westminster. The loss of its monopoly on trade from India in 1813 also increased the pressure to open up its exclusive China trade. However, the Company successfully managed to argue that the difficulty of dealing with the Chinese would be exacerbated by a commercial free-for-all, and that the tea trade might collapse; since government was as much addicted to the revenues from tea duties as the nation was to the beverage itself, disruption of the flow of tea was unthinkable to both. The fiasco of the Amherst Mission in 1816 ironically strengthened the Company's hand in this respect, as did the Chinese habit of finishing most diplomatic communications with 'Tremble fearfully hereat. Instantly obey'.

However, it was also plain from the number of nationalities and companies trading out of Canton that it was perfectly possible to do business with China without the benefit of a monopoly. During the 1820s, there was furious debate in and out of parliament concerning the continuation of the Company's monopoly on the China trade, and with the renewal of the its Charter due in 1833, it was decided to review the Company's future role in a Select Committee. Tea was treated with due seriousness in the Committee's report; it was recognised that the nett loss on the Indian branch of the Company's activities was compensated by the profit in China; it was also felt that, along with the Company's propensity to manipulate auction prices, the

Men carrying tea bricks from Sichuan to Tibet in loads of 140 kilos over treacherous roads.

price and quality of tea shipped to England was not truly competitive; and there was no doubt that the Company's monopoly on tea hindered the wider development of trade in the East. In the event, the Company as a trading entity was doomed, and with it the monopoly on the tea trade which had, in the space of a hundred and fifty years, risen in value from nothing to thirty million pounds a year.

After this, tea could legally be imported by anyone, from any point east of the Cape of Good Hope. One enterprising merchant promptly shipped a thousand chests from Gdansk to Liverpool, having calculated that the Polish port was fifteen miles east of the official line of longitude. The men who drafted the Company's Charter in 1600 must have chuckled in their graves.

A fine export silver gilt caddy, reflecting the value placed on the tea it contained. Chinese, c. 1760.

OTHER COMMODITIES FROM CHINA

The closed nature of the Chinese Empire led to an economic quirk from which private traders were quick to benefit. Silver bullion was more highly valued in China than gold, so a simple exchange could make a substantial sum. The result was that the annual trade in China of highest value to the Company between 1720 and 1750 was not in tea, silk, porcelain or any of the items that bedeck museums around the world today, but in gold bullion. After 1750, an inevitable rebalancing of the market took place, gold exports slumped, and tea assumed its rightful place.

In the mid-eighteenth century, Chinese tutenag (zinc or spelter) and paktong (a copper, nickel and zinc alloy) all enjoyed a brief vogue in Britain. In appearance they were somewhat like silver, but did not tarnish, and were used for

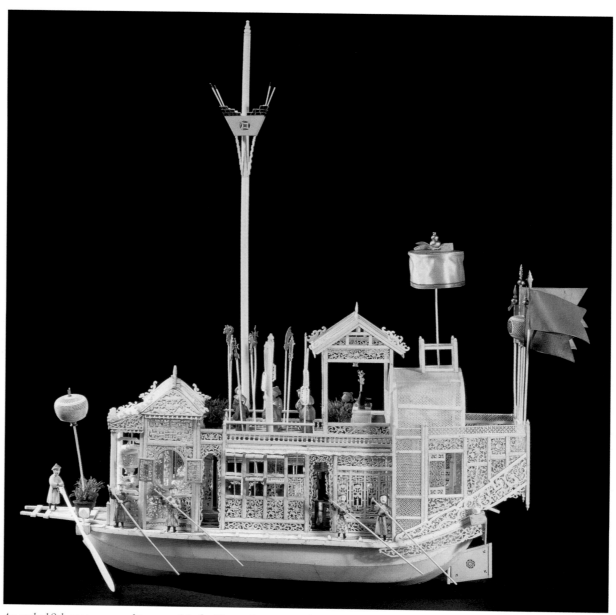

An early 19th-century carved ivory model of a Chinese boat, powered by a clockwork motor.

items such as firegrates, fenders and candlesticks. In 1760, 3,327 cwt was imported at £20 a tonne (£3327), and until 1780 an average of 20 tonnes a year was brought in. After 1780, its export from China was forbidden as it was used in combination with copper for coinage.

Lacquer, derived from resin, had been known in China since ancient times. The quality of Japanese lacquer was superior, but, fortunately for the Chinese, the Japanese were even more reticent about admitting 'foreign devils'. As a result, a small but thriving trade grew up in Chinese lacquered furniture, usually based on western designs, and mainly commissioned by private traders. This meant that work was not undertaken for stock, and the resulting haste in fulfilling orders led to a poorer quality of finish than might otherwise have been achieved.

Chinese craftsmen were skilled ivory carvers, and a substantial amount of ivory from India, southeast Asia and even Africa was shipped to Canton from earliest times. The arrival of European merchants increased the supply and the carvers, who largely worked for the substantial domestic market, began increasingly to re-export their work. Ivory

fans were made only for the export market, as were other novelty items such as the carved boat (opposite), games sets and workboxes. High quality carving was also done in mother-of-pearl and tortoiseshell.

Chinese wallpaper was popular in England throughout the eighteenth and early nineteenth century, featuring in themed Chinese rooms. These could involve as many as twenty individual panels, each hand-painted and depicting different scenes, though repeated patterns were more common. Although in value terms it was fairly insignificant, one EastIndiaman did carry back 2,236 rolls from Canton in 1775. Wallpaper manufacture was not an indigenous craft to China, but emerged from the fortuitous marriage of the skills of the Chinese in decorative painting and their use of plain paper to give walls a smooth appearance. The resultant style is still very much in evidence today, long after other aspects of Chinoiserie have lapsed into obscurity.

A fine Chinese wooden cabinet, covered with gold lacquer and oil paint decoration. Made for the export market, c. 1700.

A Chinese painted lacquer screen, c. 1750.

THE SILK TRADE

Chinese silks, like porcelain, had been known in the West long before the advent of large-scale European trading operations in southern China. From ancient times Chinese silk had been carried into the Middle East and Europe along the Silk Route through central Asia; China was also the source of the technology for harvesting the thread from cocoons of moth larvae. In the Company's time, however, Chinese silk cloth was considered inferior in quality to that of Persia and India and the bulk of the trade with China was in raw silk destined for the looms of Spitalfields in London. Some fine embroidered and painted pieces were also bought, but these never amounted to more than five per cent of the Company's annual purchases in Canton, even in the mid-eighteenth century, when exotic silks became the most fashionable of materials — both for their appearance and for their 'rustle' (silk must be the only cloth in history to be prized for auditory qualities . . .). The finer, commissioned pieces were handled by the private trade, while the Company dealt in bulk purchases. During the early nineteenth century, embroidered silk shawls with a deep knotted fringe became popular in the West, and have continued to be so.

Early 18th-century Chinese silk bed hangings recently discovered in pristine condition in boxes at Calke Abbey, Derbyshire.

From its earliest days the Company had identified silk as an alternative trading commodity, and had supplied high quality raw Persian silk from Bandar Abbas, Gombroon and Jask to Japan. Later they traded in the inferior silks of Siam and China. The Company's involvement with Japan was short-lived, but they found another market for good quality silk at home, and, until the austerity of the Cromwellian era, demand was so strong that Thomas Mun remarked in 1621 that the only commodity that the Company could not buy in sufficient quantity was Persian silk.

Lord Denbigh visited Persia and India on a Company ship in the 1620s, and this magnificent portrait of him by Van Dyck shows him in his pink silk suit, a hybrid of eastern and western styles. This is one of the earliest portraits of an English sitter dressed in native style; it was later to become fashionable in India for reasons of comfort to adopt such clothing; but to do so was frowned upon in the segregationist nineteenth century, however, except when posing for extravagant portraits.

The profitability of the silk trade led to the unlikely but successful alliance of the Company with the Persians against the Portuguese, resulting in their expulsion from the stronghold of the island of Hormuz in 1622, after which the Company enjoyed a relatively uninterrupted trade as far inland as Isfahan. The Company also encouraged the production of silks around its trading enclaves in Bengal and on the Malabar coast, which caused difficulties with the Huguenot émigré silk weavers in London, who protested that their livelihood was threatened and went as far as storming India House in the riots of 1699. Under intense lobbying, an Act was passed in 1700, prohibiting 'the use or wearing of all silks, Bengalls, and stuffs mixed with silk or herbs, of the manufacture of Persia, China or East India, and all calicoes painted, dyed, printed or stained there.'

Similar protective measures were implemented in France and Holland, but merely led to widespread smuggling. The Company itself sought to establish silk production in colonies not proscribed by the law, considering both America and the new penal colony in Botany Bay, Australia for this purpose. However, the initiative foundered.

In the meantime, Chinese silks were imported from Canton, and manufacturers there and in India began to produce designs and shapes specifically for the European market. Britain's growing wealth in the eighteenth century, combined with intense interest in the activities of the East India Company and the exotic products it traded, led to the sustained demand for silk for ties, scarves, purses, bags, dresses, shirts and ribbons, to be shown off at the fashionable spa towns of England and Scotland. The great number of lead seals bearing the East India Company's bale mark which have been recovered in excavations in the port areas of London reflects the size of this trade. Even ladies making the hazardous voyage to India in search of a husband took their finest silks with them to make sure of a catch.

One aim of the Macartney Mission to China in 1792-4 (see page 40) had been to acquire some Chinese silkworms. The mission reported that 'the Chinese, whether through Jealousy or Superstition, or both, could scarcely be persuaded to part with them'; however, the mission did acquire specimens which were successfully bred in the botanical gardens in Calcutta, that hotbed of economic botany which had been set up by the East India Company at the initiative of Sir Joseph Banks.

Trade barriers were gradually reduced between 1841 and 1846, and since then silk has been traded freely. However, it was the East India Company which was largely responsible for the development in the trade of imported silk to England, and which also greatly influenced the designs and patterns which became fashionable.

Van Dyck's portrait of William Fielding, 1st Earl of Denbigh, dressed in Indian costume, setting the trend for future paintings.

THE INDIAN PRESIDENCIES

'The Grandest Society of Merchants in the Universe.'

Anon

The three principal centres of the Company's trade and, later, its administration in India – Bombay, Madras and Calcutta – were known as the Presidencies. Each Presidency had a governor, but after the arrival of Warren Hastings, the Fort William (Calcutta) Presidency took precedence, and Hastings became the first Governor General in 1774.

MADRAS

Ceded by treaty in 1639, Madras was the first permanent toehold that the Company gained on the subcontinent. It had few natural advantages, apart from its location on the supposed site of St Thomas's martyrdom and a reasonably healthy climate, and its relationship with the Bay of Bengal was distinctly uneasy. Although it was a vital sea link with England, it was a Presidency looking for a port, for its landing facilities were rudimentary to non-existent; ships had to weigh anchor far from a shingle beach, and, furthermore, the sea was rarely calm. The standard Madras landing throughout the Company's rule went as follows: EastIndiaman moors out to sea; passengers prepare to board native outriggers which have rowed out through the rollers; ladies modestly avert eyes from eight near-naked boatmen; price negotiated for landing; passengers and luggage loaded; boat thrown around in waves; price renegotiated upwards; hair-raising final surge through the surf; passengers and luggage deposited damply on beach; first unbelieving glimpse of the classical buildings of the city,

The port of Calcutta across the Hooghli River from Kiddapore. The river was notorious for its treacherous sandbanks and tides.

CHAPTER V

The palatial residence of a European gentleman in the fashionable neo-classical style. Madras, 1850s.

glistening white with a stucco made from burnt seashells. This account is repeated time after time, with only minor variations, between the mid-seventeenth and mid-nineteenth centuries. Only after the Company left did the Government start to build a proper pier.

Madras was the Company's first fortified settlement in India; the construction of Fort St George began in 1640 and continued on and off for another 150 years. It housed all the administrative and military necessities, as well as St Mary's church (the oldest Anglican church in India), finished in 1680. The Old College, the equivalent of the Writers' Building in Calcutta (see page 169), was one of the Company's few eighteenth-century buildings in the gothic style, and still stands. At first, the Indians huddled in a separate settlement called, with startling originality, Black Town. Eventually, as the city expanded, Black Town became a desirable location for white businesses.

The merchants' town houses were more eccentric than their counterparts in Calcutta, though no less grand; they might sport long curved verandahs, odd towers and unex-

The pier at Madras under construction in the 1860s. During the Company's time, passengers and cargo endured rough landings on the beach.

plained cupolas. In the nineteenth century, Lord Clive 2nd (son of Robert Clive) forsook the security that the fortress walls provided, and built his new palace overlooking the ocean, with generous verandahs and broad terraces contributing to an air of proprietorial contentment. Merchants' houses began to spring up in the countryside away from the sea.

It was from Madras that the Company made its first significant move to become a territorial power. The French Compagnie des Indes, down the coast at Pondicherry, was initially purely a trading rival, but under the leadership of the Governor, Dupleix, it had started to forge strategic alliances with local potentates in an attempt to gain control of the Carnatic coast and oust the English. However, Mohammed Ali Wallahjah, a claimant to the throne of Arcot, ruler of the Carnatic Province, allied himself with the Company against the French and their client, the Nizam of Hyderabad. Mohammed Ali seized Trichinopoly, a key fortress in the south, where he was besieged by the French and their Indian allies. Robert Clive, then a young and ambitious writer (see chapters 6, 9 and 12) in the Company's Madras service, had requested a move to the military, and with Major Stringer Lawrence, an experienced former soldier who had been hired by the Company to run military matters out of Madras, had successfully defeated the French forces at Arcot. Their move to relieve the siege at Trichinopoly was likewise successful, and effectively ended

French ambitions in the Carnatic. (Their protégé, Chanda Sahib, was executed and lies buried at the foot of the rock.)

Dupleix had, however, come close to breaking the Company's hold, and the French could well have become the dominant power in India. Nevertheless, although French adventurers such as Benoit de Boigne continued to appear in India from time to time, often in the service of Mahratta chiefs or others opposed to the Company, no coherent European threat to the Company's position ever re-emerged.

Madras lost its pre-eminent status to Calcutta after the battle of Plassey in 1757, but the Madras army throughout the nineteenth century was admired for the quality of its arms and smartness of its uniforms, and the regimental pride amongst its sepoys was supposed to have contributed to the total absence of trouble in the Madras army during the Mutiny of 1857.

BOMBAY

Charles II had acquired Bombay, along with the habit of drinking tea, by marrying Catherine of Braganza, and the Company was delighted when the King leased it to them in 1668 for an annual rent of £10. Of the three Presidencies, Bombay was blessed with the best harbour, the finest situation (its name derived from the Portuguese 'Bom Bahia', or 'beautiful bay') and an 'unveryhealthful' climate, which meant that a Company factor could look forward to surviving two monsoons if he was lucky. The Presidency had a faltering start in its first few years, with problems of mutinous troops and warring governors, but by the end of the century it had settled comfortably into its backwater ways.

Bombay was wholly under the Company's control and this led to most of the English decamping from Surat; they were soon joined by the wealthy Gujerati and Parsee mer-

The Company's barracks and the Rock at Trichinopoly, near Madras, where Chanda Sahib lies buried along with French ambitions.

A typical Madras landing, subject of many descriptions in words and pictures.

chant communities, which were finding that the increasingly unstable political position around Surat made business difficult. Nonetheless, Bombay remained the least important of the three Presidencies, and its boom came at the end of the nineteenth century, after the Company had left. Marooned behind the Western Ghats, it was protected from the cut and thrust of Bengal adventurism and Madras's fights against the French. It made a misguided attempt at territorial expansion with a campaign against the Mahrattas, which ended in humiliation, and when they eventually made peace, Bombay turned its back on India and looked to the sea.

Always the most cosmopolitan of the Presidencies, Bombay had links with the Middle East and that region's ancient trading networks. The small but dynamic Parsee population existed on more equal terms with the English than the Indians elsewhere, and the town's agreeable situation meant that the wealthier Company servants could move out to live among the coconut groves, or in the Malabar Hills where the Governor kept a country house three miles from the city proper. A popular day out in Bombay consisted of a trip to Elephanta Island in the harbour, where the Great Cave is a shrine dedicated to Shiva. (The pillars had been damaged during the Portuguese occupation, when naval gunners respectfully used them for target practice.)

Fort William in Calcutta. Designed to prevent a recurrence of the Black Hole catastrophe, it was never taken.

Bombay, like the other Presidencies, had its fort – in this case, the Castle – and an army to go with it, but its unique feature was the Bombay Marine. The Company's navy was founded at the beginning of the eighteenth century to protect shipping against the predations of the maritime Mahratta states along the Konkan coast between Bombay and Goa, as well as the ever-present pirates. It used locally-built ships as well as British ones, and eventually built up a fleet sufficiently powerful to be able to go into action anywhere between the Red Sea and China; by 1857, the Company had 43 warships and 273 European officers. It encouraged its officers to train in hydrographic skills, which assisted the expansions of the Company's trading network, especially in the Far East. Traditionally, historians have focused on the activities of Clive in Madras and later Bengal as the start of the Company's raj, but the steady build up of the Bombay Marine, and its actions against Mahratta vessels, established the Company's first real power base in India.

Bombay Castle from the sea. The fine natural harbour of the Presidency was one of its principal advantages. Note the Company's ensign.

New commercial opportunities came with the opening up of trade in India and China, and a number of foreign traders began to move into Bombay; conspicuous among these was the Sassoon family, originally Baghdadi Jews, whose interests spread to Bombay and then China, where they dealt in the tried and tested combination of cotton and opium. They amassed a considerable fortune, and one son set up in England in 1858, buying Ashley Park in Surrey, once the seat of the Fletcher family, themselves old Company hands. The cycle was complete when Queen Victoria knighted Sir Albert Abdullah Sassoon, 1st Baronet of Kensington Gore.

CALCUTTA

Calcutta was founded by Job Charnock, the Company's most experienced factor in Bengal, in 1690, Bengal having become increasingly important to the Company's trade. Several factories had been established there since the 1640s, including one at Hooghli, just north of Calcutta. In the Moghul War, one of the Company's more absurd attempts to flex its muscle in defence of trade, Charnock had led the 308 troops sent to Bengal. Having evacuated Hooghli and its saltpetre stocks, he set up camp near the village of Kalighat where, beset by Moghul cavalry and ships, he was finally relieved by the unexpected appearance of the Bengal fleet from London. In the subsequent peace, trial factories were set up at Ulubari, Calcutta and, at the insistence of the Directors in London, Chittagong. Finally, Charnock moved back to Calcutta and posterity.

On the face of it, Calcutta seems an odd choice. The shifting sands of the treacherous tidal Hooghli river made it difficult to find an easy passage for ocean-going ships, and it was too far downriver from the centres of Bengali trade. What it did offer, in its very lack of obvious advantages, was some guarantee that trade would not be interrupted, and that more than anything else made it possible for the nascent Calcutta to establish the infrastructure and attract the people crucial to successful trade; moneylenders, munshis (translators), servants, 'chummeries' (boarding houses for bachelors), a church, a jail, warehouses and, above all, a fort. Work began on Fort William in 1697; it was to become the largest and, eventually, the most impregnable of the Company's buildings in India.

The Farquharsons' residence in Calcutta. The wealth of the Company's servants was reflected in their houses.

Government House

The finest public building in India was Government House, modelled on Keddleston Hall in Derbyshire and built at the instigation of the ambitious Governor General Richard Wellesley at the beginning of the nineteenth century. Wellesley's friend and supporter, Lord Valentia, pronounced that India should be ruled from a palace not a counting house, 'with the ideas of a Prince, not those of a retail trader in muslins and indigo'. However, the traders in muslins and indigo, also known as the Court of Directors of the East India Company, had to foot the bill for these princely pretensions, which at £67,359 was enough to precipitate Wellesley's recall. The glorious neo-classical facade was precisely that: like those of other buildings in Calcutta, the columns of Government House were not the gleaming marble they appeared to be. Lord Curzon, Viceroy in a later age, had been brought up in the original Keddleston Hall, and remarked with dry viceregal wit that whilst the pillars of one were of alabaster, the pillars of the other were lath and plaster.

Poor materials and the effects of the climate on the buildings often brought problems; Calcutta's proud new Town Hall collapsed before it was even finished in 1809, and the ballroom floor of its replacement sprang well beyond the requirements of convention. Construction difficulties were in part caused by sun-baked kutcha bricks which were prone to dissolving in the all-too-common heavy rains. Oven-baked pukka bricks were scarce and expensive. Brick awareness was so universal that the words 'kutcha' and 'pukka' entered the Anglo-Indian language to describe opposite ends of the spectrum of everything — servants, carriages, clothes, thieves, positions and even sahibs — and, perhaps inevitably, a building made of pukka bricks but held together with cutcha mud was dubbed a 'kutcha-pukka'.

The original plan had been to connect Government House by a grand avenue a mere fourteen miles long to a country house at Barrackpore. Wellesley's recall did for the avenue, but the country house was built in an estate dotted with ponds, follies, ornamental bridges and monuments.

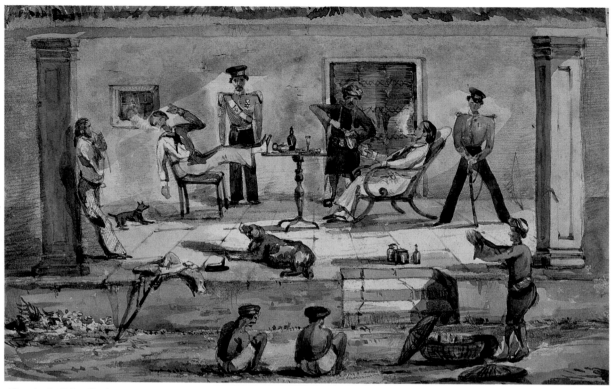

After the Ball: 'griffins' (newcomers to India) relaxing in their 'chummery' (bachelor lodgings) in Calcutta.

Population of Calcutta in 1837

Arabs	351
Armenians	636
Chinese	362
English	3,138
Eurasians	4,746
French	160
Hindus	137,651
Jews	307
Low Castes	19,084
Moghuls	509
Muslims	58,744
Portuguese	3,190
Thugs	683
TOTAL	**229,561**

Whilst Government House outshone them all, the Calcutta town houses of the more prosperous merchants in turn dwarfed their London counterparts, with vast drawing rooms, verandahs, public rooms and private sitting rooms. The social life of the Company's servants was both glittering and glistening; the convention of wearing clothes suited to home in a climate suited to none made dancing a quadrille a sticky experience.

Rivalries between the Presidencies were intense, if light-hearted. One of the authors of *Hobson-Jobson* recalls meeting a troop of the Royal Bombay Fusiliers at Aden, on his way to Bengal. He was told that the main problems of his Calcutta Presidency were: 'first the inferiority of the Bengal Horse Artillery system; second that the Bengalees were guilty of the base effeminacy of drinking beer out of champagne glasses; third that in pig-sticking they threw the spear at the boar.'

An overheated sahib is hosed down in preparation for his appearance at a Calcutta Fancy dress ball.

by Sir Charles Doyley Bart

COMPANY AT HOME

'*A corporation of men with long heads and deep purposes.*'

Ned Ward c.1690

STRUCTURE AND STOCK

In 1709, the Company was forced by parliament to merge with a rival company, the cheekily-titled 'New East India Company', which had been encroaching on its monopoly. The merged entity was called 'The United Company of Merchants of England Trading to the East Indies' and was granted a new Coat of Arms in recognition of the change. Other than that, the Company's structure remained remarkably unchanged throughout its existence.

Despite its importance to the nation's welfare, and the preoccupation of many politicians with its affairs, the East India Company was just that – a company, with stock-holders, dividends, directors, articles of association and all the usual trappings of corporate governance. The Court of Proprietors met quarterly, or called an extraordinary meeting if necessary; in spring, they voted on a dividend recommended by the Court of Directors. The Directors were City merchants, rarely actually in the service of the Company, and were themselves elected by Proprietors with more than £200 (in the early years), later £500, worth of stock.

Once over the £500 threshold, and regardless of the number of shares held, a Proprietor could cast only one vote. It took a man of the ingenuity of Clive to realise that it was more advantageous to hold a number of £500 blocks through nominees than to hold a larger concentration in his own name.

The General Court Room in session c. 1820. Clive and others influence proceedings posthumously.

CHAPTER VI

Clive had his eyes on control of the Company, but he was not the only one. Warren Hastings' invaluable agent and ally in London, Lachlan Macleane, had also hatched an ambitious plan to acquire all the East India Company stock himself, but it came to nothing.

The value of the Company stock was prone to wild fluctuations, particularly in the 1760s when Clive, as well as manipulating the voting rights and secretly buying stock himself, was back in India securing the 'diwani' (tax revenues) of Bengal and setting up a new, supposedly uncorrupt regime. Clive's prediction that the diwani would produce £2 million in annual revenue surplus led to a one hundred per cent rise in the price of Company stock. However, the Bengal famine of 1770, which caused the collapse of the predicted revenues, precipitated a disastrous fall in the value of the stock, resulting in the suspension of dividends and a request by the Company to government for a £1 million loan.

The Regulating Act of 1773 was part of a package of reforms to stave off the Company's imminent bankruptcy. It imposed new rules of corporate governance on Directors and stockholders, as well as creating the Council in Calcutta which so bedevilled Hastings' attempts to straighten out the Company's affairs (see page 99). Pitt's India Act of 1784 – again a response to a crisis in the Company's finances – created a Board of Control, with six members, including the Chancellor and a Secretary of State, who were to direct the Court of Directors. This saw the end of the Company's independence from government; however, it remained in control of its commercial operations, and the monopoly on the China trade, with its all-important tea revenues, remained intact.

Parliament's termination of the Company's monopoly on the Indian trade in 1813, and its opening up to competition recognised that the Company's interests in India were now principally those of a ruler (under the supervision of the Crown). The Charter Act of 1833 formally ended both the Company's trading monopoly with China and all trading rights in India; trading was deemed to be incompatible with ruling.

It is ironic that the Company, founded for the express purpose of trade, had become, in violation of its Charter and the wishes of its Directors, de facto ruler of large swathes of India, and spent its last twenty-five years deprived of its trading activities and authorised to carry out only that function of governance for which it had not been created, and for which few thought it fit.

The anomaly was not unobserved at the time. In a parliamentary debate, Thomas Macaulay remarked: 'A society [the Company] which judging a priori from its constitution was as little suited for the imperial function as the Merchant Taylors' Company or the New River Company, was exer-

The South Sea Bubble

The infamous bursting of the South Sea Bubble in 1720 – the crash of a company set up in the mould of the East India Company but focusing on trade in Spanish South America – had an adverse effect on the investment climate of both the City and of northern Europe, as well as bankrupting numerous individuals. These porcelain plates were produced for the Dutch market and contained cautionary inscriptions, lest Dutch speculators be tempted to follow suit.

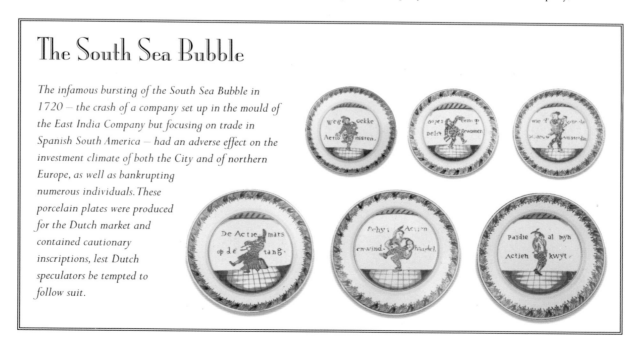

cising sovereignty over more people, with a larger revenue and a larger army than that under the direct control of the executive government of the United Kingdom.' It was not until 1858, in the aftermath of the Mutiny, that the Company 'little suited for the imperial function' finally handed over that imperial function to the Crown.

BUSINESS OPERATIONS

To finance its first Voyage, the Company raised subscription capital of £68,373, and the subsequent eleven Voyages likewise raised money according to their requirements — between £7,000 and £80,000. Sometimes profits could be spectacular (the Third Voyage made a return of 234 per cent for its subscribers) though often they were not. When, increasingly, it was found necessary to retain subscription

The Chairman's Chair, with the Coat of Arms of the United Company. Early 18th century.

money from one Voyage to finance the next, it soon became appropriate to formalise this in a more stable structure through the issue of joint stock. The Company was one of the first in England to do this, and it helped to attract a different sort of investor — one who was after long-term capital gain and annual dividends, rather than a fast turnaround at a substantial profit. The first joint stock issue, in 1613, raised £420,436. The Company had by then exported £320,000 worth of goods, and spent £360,000 purchasing goods in the East, which had been sold for £2,044,600. Even after shipping costs had been deducted, it produced a healthy balance sheet.

By 1682, total paid-up capital had reached £739,782, and after 1714 it stabilised at just over £3,000,000. Borrowings on short-term bonds were made throughout the period.

The way that the Company conducted its business is surprisingly familiar. Meetings of the Court of Directors were recorded in the Court minutes (the equivalent of the board minutes of a modern company), in which the key collective corporate, strategic and operational decisions were recorded, after being discussed and, if necessary, voted on. The minutes would include details of the auction results which were key to the financial health of the Company. Today, sales figures would be reported in a similar way, although they would not be included in the minutes; indeed, after 1709, auction results for the Company were recorded separately.

Important day-to-day functions were carried out by the Committee of Correspondence, which comprised five or six Directors. Their role was partly that of a buying department, partly general administration. They were responsible for placing orders for the purchase of goods with the commanders (captains) or Supercargoes of EastIndiamen bound for the Orient. They would write their orders in the despatch book, which also noted particular requirements such as, in the case of tea, 'Be very careful that the wood of the chests . . . be well seasoned and has no scent.' (Tea merchants to this day are very concerned about 'taint', that is, when a powerful alien odour is absorbed by the tea, and the flavour ruined as a result.) The Committee of Correspondence also maintained records of all letters and instructions sent to the factories and Presidencies.

Copies of the despatch book orders would then be forwarded to the EastIndiamen, and when the ships arrived at their chosen destination, their purchase requirements would be implemented by a council set up by the

The Court of Directors of the East India Company. Comfortable chairs and inspirational paintings are much in evidence.

Company. Their decisions would be recorded in a journal. Councillors, like the commanders of the ships and their crew, were able to benefit from an allocation, based on seniority, of 'private trade' space in the ships. One of the reasons that the Company prospered over its European rivals, especially the Dutch, was that the Directors effectively institutionalised the corruption of its servants by allowing and regulating the conduct of this private trade. This gave Company servants a substantial financial incentive, which compensated significantly for modest salaries and dangerous conditions. A commander might easily earn ten times his annual salary of £120 through private trade.

Upon return to London, the goods would be warehoused and an auction catalogue prepared. Private traders had to auction goods through the Company, and paid a fifteen per cent surcharge. If a private trader had fulfilled a specific order, such as for armorial porcelain, then the value was assessed by the Company and the premium charged on that. The auctions were always conducted by a Director in the Sale Room at East India House in Leadenhall Street in the City – the 'howling and yelling' was such that the proceedings could often be heard through the stone walls. In the case of tea, dealers such as Richard Knight, whose business card is illustrated, bought tea from the Company at auction and distributed it to independent retailers. The auction results provided the Directors and the Committee of Correspondence with information regarding the profitability of the commodities they had imported, and the process started over again.

Both the Company and private traders became increasingly sophisticated, particularly in relation to the China trade in porcelain, carved ivory, furniture and other goods, providing samples to show potential customers. The Company showed enough innovative spirit to try to create demand where there was none; the glass market in England was dominated by the Glass Sellers' Company, and the importation of porcelain wine flutes was an (unsuccessful) attempt to circumvent that powerful monopoly.

Like a modern corporation, the Company made use of gifts as a way of influencing people. The Company's Charter required regular renewal, and members of the royal family received particular attention – none more so than Charles II, who had established a menagerie of rare and exotic animals and birds in Birdcage Walk, St James's Park. He expected the East India Company to present him with new specimens each time a ship returned from the East. When, in 1664, a returning captain reported to the Court of Directors that their agents in the East Indies had failed to make provision for the King, they scoured the ship for a suitable gift, and the minute book records: 'The Governour acquainting ye Court that ye Factors haveing in every place failed ye company of such

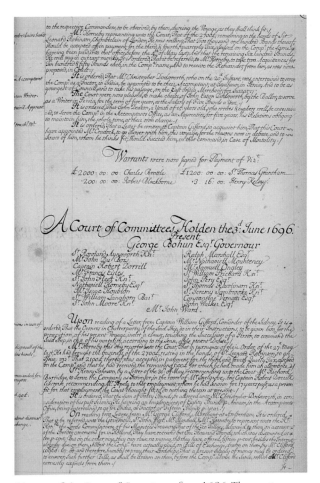

Minutes of the Court of Committees from 1696. The meeting was chaired by the Governor, George Bohun.

The business card of Richard Knight, a wholesaler of tea bought at auction from the Company.

things as they writt for to have presented his majesty with and that his majesty might not find himself wholly neglected by ye company, he was of the opinion if ye Court thinck fitt that a silver case of oile of cinnamon and some good tea, be provided for that end.' This was the first time that the king received tea from the Company, and within weeks of this gift being made, the Company ordered a hundred pounds of the 'best tee procurable' from its Bantam factory, which suggests that it had been favourably received.

Shortly before this, the Directors had themselves conducted a tea tasting, and had decided that 'good tea was to be provided for the Company's occassions'. A Mr and Mrs Harris had been appointed beadle and housekeeper at the Company's headquarters in 1661, and Mrs Harris took charge of brewing tea for committee meetings. She was com-

East India Docks soon after their completion. The masthouse, clearly visible, was a technological triumph.

The docks with the Thames and Greenwich beyond. The smaller dock to the left of the masthouse was for outgoing Indiamen.

pensated for the loss of four silver spoons in 1666, and would have been the first to brew tea in the silver teapot (see page 69) presented to his fellow Directors by Lord Berkeley in 1670. Those hallowed traditions of English business, the tea lady and tea break, owed their genesis, appropriately enough, to the company that first imported tea.

WAREHOUSES, DOCKS AND SHIPBUILDING

Initially the Company leased ships and worked them hard – three of the four ships of the First Voyage made the Third Voyage as well. Growing international trade increased demand for ocean-going vessels, and this kept the ship-building prices high. From 1607, the Company built their own ships in Deptford (the scene of Marlowe's murder and of Peter the Great's lessons in shipbuilding). This enabled them to cut building costs by three quarters, and to invest heavily in fitting out three new ships for the Sixth Voyage at a total cost of £82,000. One of them, the *Trades' Increase,* was, at 1293 tonnes, the largest vessel ever to have been built in England, but the vessel was an unwieldy failure that ended its days as a burnt-out, rotting hulk in Bantam.

The docks at Deptford had been used from the first for warehousing and provisioning the Company's vessels, and by 1610 over 500 men worked there. Expansion continued apace, and the Company soon owned and ran twenty-one ships – the largest private fleet in England. Additional yards were opened at Blackwall, and by 1621 the Company had built 10,000 tonnes of shipping, and employed 2,500 seamen. The Deptford (1643) and Blackwall (1650) yards were later sold to private shipbuilders, although the Company continued to use them for repairs and provisioning.

The scale and complexity of the operation can be judged by the responsibilities of William Burrell, employed by the Company until his dismissal in 1625 for malpractice. Burrell organised and controlled the different operations of the yards, designed the ships – even personally going to the forest to choose the timber – designed and built wet and dry docks, wharves, warehouses and workshops, ran a foundry for anchors, nails and chains, a spinning shed for cordage and sails, a slaughter house, a salting house, and a powder mill for the manufacture of gunpowder (using saltpetre bought back from Surat). He was also responsible for paying his workers and for their food and work clothes.

Shipyards were also developed in India, to build to Company specification. One of the last of the Company ships, the *Edwin Fox*, was built in Bengal in 1853. The ship was leased by the government for use in the Crimean War, then used to transport convicts to Australia, and later to carry immigrants to New Zealand, where it still lies.

Initially the Company's ships unloaded in the City of London (between Tower Bridge and London Bridge today) with the City's other maritime traffic. Goods were then taken for warehousing to East India House or to leased space nearby. As the average size of EastIndiamen increased in the second half of the eighteenth century (to 1,000 tonnes or more), ships had to anchor in deeper water down-river at Blackwall, and then their cargoes were unloaded into lighters. It made sense for the Company to commission a dock for its exclusive use from the East India Dock Company, which had been established for just this purpose. Opened in 1806, the dock was a model of modernity. The masthouse enabled an Indiaman to be fully rigged in a matter of days rather than weeks, and the landing facilities were greatly improved. Pepper warehouses and spice-grinding operations sprang up around the docks, when it was realised that ground spices were easier and cheaper to transport for the home market.

The sheer volume of tea arriving in the country and going into storage put great pressure on the Company's Cutler Street warehouses in the City, already covering five acres and employing 4,000 warehousemen and 400 clerks. When its tea monopoly eventually collapsed, the Company put 30 acres of warehouses up for auction. These were bought for £370,000, considerably less than their cost.

A CHAPEL AND SOME MEMORIALS

The Company built a chapel in Poplar, near to the Blackwall yard, in a field behind its hospital for sick and injured sailors. It was one of only three churches built during Cromwell's Commonwealth, and is unusually open and light in design, but with a suitably puritan absence of deco-ration, apart from the Company's Coat of Arms in a ceiling boss. The eight pillars of the nave are made from the wooden masts of Company ships. The design, though unspectacular, has an austere elegance, and influenced that of many of the red brick churches built on the north-east-ern seaboard of America, especially Virginia, before Wren's

church designs became the favoured model. The church-yard of Poplar chapel (now St Matthias) contains many overgrown and decayed gravestones of long-forgotten servants of the Company.

In contrast, Major General Sir Eyre Coote, the military right hand of Clive in Bengal and later Commander in Chief in India, was buried in this unforgettable tomb in Westminster Abbey. Like many officers of the Indian Army, he was of Irish stock, the son of a clergyman. As well as playing a decisive part at Plassey, he drove the French out of India with the victory at Wandewash in 1759, and was thus, along with Clive, one of the true founders of the Company's raj in the subcontinent.

A statue of Sir Charles James Napier stands close to, albeit dwarfed by, Nelson's column in Trafalgar Square. Napier, with true Company insouciance, had taken Sind while on a mission to assist the orderly withdrawal from Khandahar of the remains of the Army of the Indus. A celebrated one-word report of his victory to the Governor General is usually attributed to him: 'Peccavi' it stated – 'I have sinned'. Sadly for posterity, however, it was revealed to have been entirely invented by a Punch cartoonist.

Napier was one of the more colourful characters of his era; a descendant of a mistress of Charles II, his mother was a great beauty, beloved by George II. His journals are full of irrepressible vitality – even at the time of the Sind campaign, when he was in his sixties, he felt he should try keep himself in check: 'Charles! Charles Napier! – Take heed of your ambition for military glory; you had scotched that snake, but this high command will, unless you are careful, give it all its vigour again. Get thee behind me Satan!' Satan, however, does not take a back seat for long: 'How is all this to end? We have no right to seize Scinde; yet we shall do so, and a very advantageous, useful, humane piece of rascality it will be.' He was one of the first commanders to warn of the increasing alienation of the sepoys in the run up to the Mutiny (see page 175), and at his suggestion common soldiers were stationed in the hills for the good of their health. The affection with which he was held by his men is reflected in the inscription on his memorial, erected by public subscription, 'the most numerous contributors being private soldiers'.

The admirably understated tomb of Major General Sir Eyre Coote in Westminster Abbey, donated by the Company.

An inscribed silver teapot presented to the Directors of the Company by Lord Berkeley in 1670.

FROM COFFEE HOUSE TO TEA GARDEN

Whilst the Company was busy trading coffee to Persia and Surat in the 1620s, western Europe remained in almost total ignorance of the charms of the beverage. However, those involved in the East India Company were in a position to anticipate the coming trend; Thomas Garraway, a relation of Sir Henry Garraway, Governor of the Company in 1639, opened one of London's most famous coffee houses, Garraway's, in Cornhill, and was the first man in England to serve and retail tea.

The Company began to bring significant quantities of coffee into England after 1660, undercutting the prices of the rival Levant Company which bought coffee from the entrepôts of Smyrna and Aleppo. Detailed records of the Company's auctions survive from 1664 onwards, and in March 1788 the value of coffee sold was £63,597 – half as much again as chinaware, although only a tenth of the value of tea. By this stage the rival East Indies companies of France and Holland had been wound up, and thus the East India Company enjoyed a thriving re-export trade, through intermediaries, of coffee to Europe and the United States.

'The East offering her riches to Brittania', a painted ceiling from East India House currently on display in the Foreign Office.

The London coffee house boom of 1650 to 1750 coincided with the development of many of the City of London institutions in part designed to service the burgeoning East India Company trade. It was common practice for the news of ships travelling back from the East to be relayed to a coffee house named Lloyds (first in Tower Street and later on the corner of Lombard Street), where those with maritime interests were to be found. A fledgling marine insurance business started there, which grew to be the world's largest insurance company. Likewise, Jonathan's in Change Alley was the meeting place for those with an interest in transactions in companies and shares, and from it grew the Stock Exchange where, until its closure, the messengers were still called waiters. Coffee shops abounded in London – there may have been as many as three hundred by 1720 – and spread to the provincial cities. The East India Company's own imports of coffee met the demand for this fashionable new beverage, and, in turn, created further demand through the businesses that sprang up around this new trading good. The very nature of coffee caught a certain mood in the City; stimulating, intellectual and subversive, coffee fuelled the rise of trade and capitalism. After 1750, tea ruled supreme in England, as coffee house gave way to drawing room. Tea also caught the spirit of its times – a more prosperous, domestic and elegant era reflected by, and reflecting the contemplative, feminine 'ying' qualities of the beverage.

East India House

The Company's most important building was, of course, East India House. For the first fifty years, the Company headquartered in the houses of various City merchants, then acquired Craven House on Leadenhall Street, a half-timbered Elizabethan mansion. It was quickly decorated to demonstrate the Company's intent: a painting of a fleet of merchantmen was topped by a wooden statue of a sailor between two dolphins. Over the next two hundred years the renamed East India House underwent extensive remodelling and expansion to the rear, to create rooms befitting the ever-increasing status of the Company, and to provide an auction or Sale Room.

Although they were loath to spend money on fripperies, preferring to rely on gifts, the Directors occasionally commissioned paintings or sculptures of its most celebrated servants to dignify proceedings; the conduct of the General Court Room was overseen by statues of Robert Clive, Stringer Lawrence, Admiral Pocock, Coote and Cornwallis. Company paintings decorated the Court of Directors' room, and suitably regal chairs were made for their illustrious behinds.

The final remodelling and extension at the end of the eighteenth century was in strictly classical mode (below), imposingly porched and pedimented.

Not a trace of the Company's Asian dealings was allowed to creep into the exterior, and although a new library and museum was created to house the oriental manuscripts, pictures and objects that flowed into the Company's possession, all the public rooms and offices of East India House retained a resolutely British appearance. Not even their trade goods — porcelain, textiles, furniture, tea — were considered suitable for display, and it was not until 1912, long after the Company and all its possession had passed to the Crown, that the Marquess of Crewe, Secretary of State for India, took the unprecedented step of hanging eleven Indian miniatures in his rooms.

Sezincote House in Oxfordshire, the finest marriage of Indian and English architecture.

THE COMPANY IN LITERATURE

Jane Austen, that quintessentially English writer, was not untouched by events in India; her brother Francis was an admiral stationed in the China Seas during the 1840s. More mysteriously, a beautiful young heiress, known to her as Cousin Eliza and rumoured to be an illegitimate daughter of Warren Hastings, married one of Jane's brothers after her first husband had been executed in the French revolution. Cousin Eliza's mother, Jane's aunt Philadelphia, had gone to India with the 'Fishing Fleet' and had hooked Tysoe Hancock, a respectable but dull man. She was believed to have caught the eye of Hastings (whose passion for, and loyalty to his wife Marian was nonetheless legendary), and Eliza was the result; her £10,000 was said to be her share of the Hastings' £170,000 fortune.

Yet Austen's novels make little mention of India, except to provide an exotic location in which characters such as Colonel Brandon in *Sense and Sensibility* can pine mysteriously:

'. . . he [Brandon] has always answered my enquiries with the readiness of good breeding and good nature.'

'That is to say,' cried Marianne contemptuously, 'he has told you that in the East Indies the climate is hot, and the mosquitoes are troublesome.'

. . . 'Perhaps,' said Willoughby, 'his observations may have extended to the existence of Nabobs, gold mohrs, and palanquins.'

Cousin Eliza's tale would have made rich source material for the author of *Fanny Hill: Memoirs of a Woman of Pleasure.*

John Cleland's erotic masterpiece may have been influenced by his thirteen years spent in the Company's legal department in Bombay. Certainly, the Indies play a crucial role in separating our eponymous heroine from Charles, her true love, who leaves the action for most of the book on a voyage to recover the fortune left to him by an uncle 'at one of the factories in the South-Seas'.

John Wordsworth, brother of the poet William, had a long and distinguished service with the merchant fleet of the Company. His adventurous life made it impossible for him to marry Mary Hutchinson, and she later married William. One of John's aims was to free William from financial responsibilities so that he could concentrate on poetry, and he was liberal with his gifts. In 1800, he took command of the *Earl of Abergavenny*, which went down in 1805 off Portland Bill. John remained at his post; his last words were 'Let her go – and God's will be done,' to the first mate. William, and John's friends, who included William Wilberforce, were distraught.

THE NABOB

> **'General Clive has arrived, all over estates and diamonds.'**
>
> Horace Walpole, 1758

The Nabobs – men returning with vast fortunes made in India – attracted considerable enmity, particularly from the English aristocracy, not least because of their irritating, if understandable habit of setting themselves up like

The Snake Garden at Sezincote House, showing the Hindu-inspired lingam.

the country noblemen they conspicuously were not. It must have seemed like the end of civilisation to her when the Dowager Duchess of Newcastle sold her Claremont estate in Surrey to her late husband's former protégé, Robert Clive, especially as he had the effrontery to beat her down from £40,000 to £25,000. Pitt the Elder railed against the Nabobs: 'Without connections, without any natural interest in the soil, the importers of foreign gold forced their way into parliament by such a torrent of corruption, as no private hereditary fortune can resist.' (Fighting talk from a man whose family fortunes were founded on interloping and a dubious diamond deal by his grandfather in Madras . . .).

Nabobs (a corruption of the Hindi word 'nawab' – a Muslim landowner or ruling prince) were frequently cultivated men, but, as far as the Establishment was concerned, they were, like the comparably wealthy northern industrialists who were to shortly arrive down the historical pipeline, tainted by trade, and rather dubious trade at that. The press made the most of their supposed parvenu pretensions, and their enormous riches of mysterious and exotic provenance provided colourful subject matter for the caricaturists of the time.

More serious were the political ramifications. India had assumed much greater strategic and economic importance as a result of the activities of these same Nabobs, and the political establishment was anxious to protect its own actual as well as potential interests. The Nabobs threatened to form a potent political lobby by buying up 'rotten boroughs' to obtain a seat in parliament (another accoutrement of respectability, along with the estate and the town house), assuming that their experience of India was a desirable political commodity. Add to this rich mélange the increasing concerns over the American colonies, with the ensuing unseemly struggles in parliament, the Company, and even India itself: the next chaotic twenty years could be seen as the birth pangs of imperial Britain.

A TAJ IN THE ENGLISH COUNTRYSIDE

Although many of the Nabobs chose to spend their fortunes on country estates, few either remodelled or built in a style reflecting the origins of their wealth. Warren Hastings, true to form, decorated the interior of his house at Daylesford with furniture, paintings and miniatures reflecting his abiding interest in Indian culture; he also asked the architect

Count Roupee, a caricature of a Nabob, depicted riding as if to the manor born in Hyde Park.

Samuel Pepys Cockerell to add a Moghul dome to a basically classical design.

Cockerell's brother, Sir Charles Cockerell, was himself a Nabob, and in 1805 he commissioned Samuel to design him a house – Sezincote in Gloucestershire – in the Indian mould. Sir Charles had met Thomas Daniell (see page 119) in Calcutta, and retained him as a consultant to ensure authenticity. Daniell was also briefed to work with Humphry Repton, one of the foremost landscape gardeners at the end of the eighteenth century, to design the gardens, which are full of exotic and florid touches such as the Snake Pool, featuring a lingam (a phallic column frequently found in Hindu temples) surmounted by a three-headed snake.

Sezincote represents the annexation of Indian architectural ideas to the service of the English country house ideal. Although the interior remains doggedly English, the exterior of the house, with its Hindu ground floor and Moghul first floor, and a wonderful arcaded orangery, represents the finest example of an essentially English house informed by an Indian sensibility. It is interesting to note the evenhandedness with which both Muslim and Hindu features were incorporated here; the English at the time usually found Muslim architecture and people more sympathetic than their Hindu equivalents – in part ascribed to the Muslims having but one god and a holy book, whereas the Hindus had a bewildering number of terrifying gods and no single scripture.

COMPANY OVERLAND AND SEA

> *'I live ... at the devotion of the wind and seas.'*
> Captain James Lancaster

EASTINDIAMEN

The vessels known as EastIndiamen evolved during the eighteenth century as a hybrid merchant vessel and warship. At first they averaged about 500 tonnes, with 90 crew members and 30 guns, but they gradually increased in size until, by the heyday of the tea trade, they were 1,400 tonnes and carried 48 guns. They looked like warships, and were run like warships; their officers usually came from the same families as those who served in the Royal Navy.

Until the 1830s, a passenger on an EastIndiaman could expect the most luxurious voyage of any by sea, but that was relative; first-hand accounts paint a grim picture of danger and discomfort.

The threat of shipwreck remained omnipresent, and many a servant of the Company, having survived his term in India or elsewhere, died in a storm on the journey home. Tropical storms provided the most conspicuous sudden danger, but the Mozambique Channel, the Cape and even the English Channel could spring an unwelcome surprise. James Fraser was saved from the shipwreck of the *Daedalus* in 1813 off Ceylon: '. . . Still less shall I forget the silent alarming grief, the fixed tearless eye & the deranged look of Mrs Maxwell, while her husband was still on board the wreck, the anguished look when told there was no hope — and least of all shall the awful sight of the vessel going down, the beautiful ship which had borne us so long, so proudly, disappearing for ever . . .' (James Fraser, *Fraser Papers*, Bundle 439, National Register of Archives, Scotland). A

The cover page of an illustrated guide to the new overland route to India, 1842.

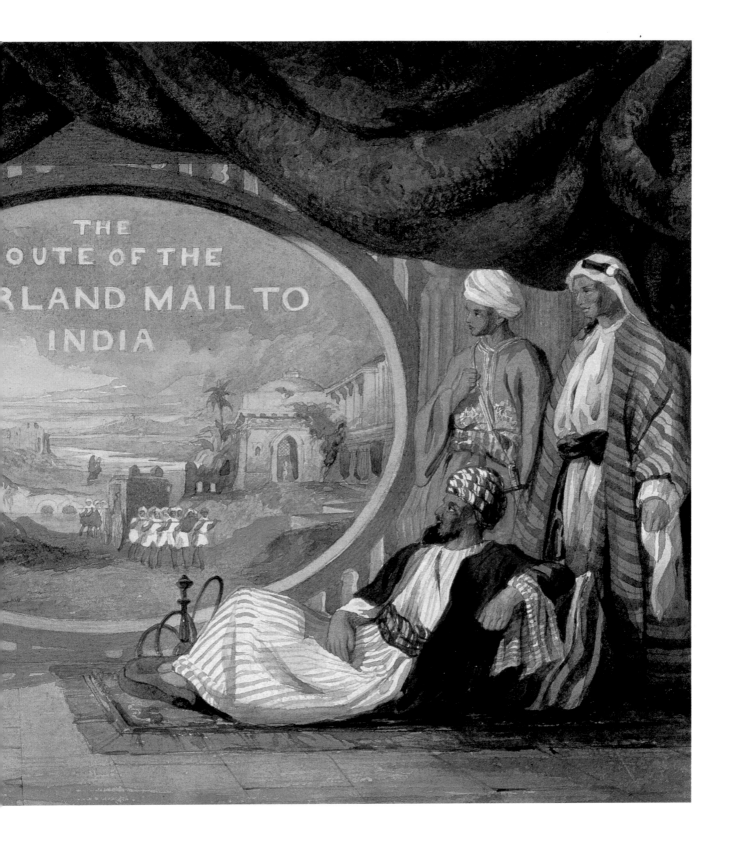

passage, and the storage space to go with it, were best negotiated personally with the commander, and passengers were advised to visit the vessel so that they knew what they were in for. The fare was settled with the purser: 'The sums paid depend entirely upon demand, their size, the ship's destination, and the circumstance of the person selling his accommodation. The several portions of the round-house and great cabin which are considered the captain's property of course are paid for in proportion to their respective dimensions' (Captain Williamson, *The East India Company Vade-Mecum*, 1810). The round-house was a cabin on the quarterdeck, but if, for want of means or space, the passenger ended up on the second deck, he was advised to keep his baggage raised to avoid a soaking, or, better still, to hang it from the beams in canvas slings or baskets.

In the early days there was no restriction on baggage, and the chief mate of the *Rainbow* complained in 1687 of a passenger 'having his moveables along with him, so that we scarce had room for our seamen and provisions'. Later,

Buttons from a Company naval uniform. The lion holding a crown was irreverently known as the 'Cat and Cheese'.

restrictions were imposed according to rank after a reported instance when a passenger returned with sixty-five tonnes of baggage. Musical instruments 'for the voyage' were allowed – a loophole which two sisters exploited to the full in 1821, one bringing a piano on board, and the other a harp.

Illness, being swept overboard, and even suicide were the causes of death listed by John MacDonald (who had had the distinction of having been present at the death of the writer, Laurence Sterne) on a voyage to India in 1771: 'Sometimes one died, and the burying was always before breakfast. At other times a man or boy would fall overboard and bury himself. A lieutenant going out as a passenger to India, wanted to do the same; but was caught hold of by the legs, and stopped from that rash action. Something troubled his mind.' Any gentleman who had not crossed the equator before was shaved with a saw and tarbrush by Mrs Neptune and her daughters, played in bawdy style by the largest sailors. Later in the voyage, the passengers were entertained by a 'fight at sea between the fleets of Hyder Ali and the Mahrattas. We saw the firing very well for two hours.' For good measure, MacDonald describes how on the return journey two men were swept overboard by a heavy sea, only to be returned to deck by the next wave. (*Memoirs of an 18th Century Footman*, Century, 1985).

The Revd Hobart Caunter describes a storm in the 1830s when the only woman passenger was swept out of her cabin by a wave which bore her into the main cabin 'head foremost . . . dripping like a mermaid, her hair hanging about her shulders in thin strips'. She was rescued by the captain, which was unusual, for captains were often the worst enemies of women on board, initiating draconian regimes which could include virtual starvation. It was quite usual for women to be forced to eat in their cabins (if they had one) because the language in the cuddy (main cabin) was so bad; Mrs Sherwood, the wife of an army officer, slept on a hammock strung above a cannon whilst bilge water slopped on the floor underneath. More lowly women would find themselves berthed next to the horses. Needless to say, quarrels amongst the passengers were rife, sometimes ending in duels between the men. Considering the priggishness of some of the passengers, that is not surprising: ' . . . am tormented every day by a parcel of gentlemen coming to the end of my berth to talk politics and smoke cheroots – advise them rather to think of mending holes in their old shirts, like me' (Hon J Lindsay, *Lives of the Lindsays*, 1781).

Women, too, were not above a good spat. Given the importance of preserving a white complexion in order to make a good catch in India, it is not surprising to find that hatboxes were vital items of baggage, and that hats were worn whatever the weather. The *Bengal Gazette* wryly reported in July 1780 that, whether through accident or altercation, a group of eleven young ladies had arrived in Calcutta without an undamaged hat to show between them.

Regardless of all else, Sunday services were conducted on board with due solemnity by the captain on a temporary altar set up on the main deck, and all passengers and crew were required to turn out in clean clothes.

PIRATES

Apart from contending with the ships of the other European East India Companies (principally those of the Dutch and the French) at sea, EastIndiamen also had to deal with pirates and interlopers. At issue was the Company's monopoly over the English eastern trade: pirates wanted to deprive the Company of the benefit of this trade by the time-honoured methods of swash and buckle; interlopers were other English merchants who resented the monopoly and wanted to circumvent it. It suited the Company to gloss over the difference between the two, especially when trying

A sailors' mess on board ship, where life for passengers was cramped and exceedingly uncomfortable.

Furniture on Board

The long voyage out to the East led to cabin furniture being developed which could either be used afterwards in the home or be sold to the next passengers taking the ship. (As Emma Roberts noted, 'little is required for the house besides the furniture which has been used for the Cabin on Board ship'.)

William Hickey described paying 8,000 rupees for his third passage home in February 1808, and 20,800 more for 'outfit in clothes, furniture for cabin, etc., including two large teakwood chests, a bureau with writing desk and apparatus, a *table and a capital cot for sleeping in'. Ordinary passengers were allowed a table, a sofa or two chairs, a washstand, and bedding. The sofa generally incorporated two drawers underneath it, and the washstand could be shut down to form a table. Coffee-making equipment, a water filter, and a supply of tea, coffee, soap and sweets were considered necessities, while medicine chests with neatly arranged rows of medicine in glass bottles, portable soup (dehydrated concentrate), soda water and perfumes travelled in fine mahogany or teak boxes.*

to justify their attacks on apparently friendly trading vessels in eastern ports. Whilst it might well have been clear to the Company that the interloper was a villainous threat to their monopoly, a Moghul official could scarcely be expected to sympathise.

Pirates were rife in the Indian Ocean, and Moghul shipowners plying the route from India to Arabia, having accepted the Company as natural heirs to the Portuguese, expected the same level of protection that their predecessors had provided. The Company had neither the resources nor the inclination to provide this protection, and piracy became a serious problem, especially in the later years of the seventeenth century.

The names of the most famous read like a schoolboy fantasy – 'The arch-pirate' Captain John Avery, Captain 'Cutlass' Culliford, Captain Dirk Shivers (the origin, perhaps, of the comic-book pirates' curse 'Shiver me timbers, ye hearties'), Captain Levasseur – but all must defer to the infamous Captain Kidd who, in defiance of the cliché as well as the Company's wishes, was a gamekeeper-turned-poacher. Hired by the Directors at the instigation of the Governor of New York to help suppress piracy, William Kidd soon discovered the most profitable side of the fence, and became the scourge of the Arabian Sea until he was caught and executed in 1701.

If piracy in the Indian Ocean was an epidemic, in the South China Sea it was a plague. For the most part then, as now, the outlaws of that sea were local Malays and Chinese, relying on the combination of fast-moving 'prahus' or junks, and impenetrable coastal jungle for advantage. Even the

Company's own servants caught the disease. One, Samuel White, was mate on a Company ship in 1675, became a factor in Madras, and next showed up in the service of the King of Siam, alternating legitimate trade with part-time pirating, whilst his former employers put a price on his head which was never redeemed. It was only when the Company's Bombay Marine introduced the armed steamship *Diana*, with its shallow draft and independence of wind, that any significant threat could be posed to these predators. Later, similar gunboats, such as the *Nemesis*, proved their worth in the Opium Wars and actions against Borneo pirates. 'Gunboat diplomacy' was effective in combating the defiance of governments; gunboats were equally effective against those who lived outside the law.

INTERLOPERS

Once the potential profit of trade with the East had been recognised, other merchants began to question the Company's right to a monopoly. The Company's reply would be that the risks attendant on such an enterprise could only be justified if the benefits were exclusively theirs, and that the national interest was best served by having a co-ordinated trade policy. Nonetheless, especially as the Indian piece trade expanded, it must have been galling for any enterprising merchant to be excluded by charter. Some simply ignored the Company's monopoly, and called at Indian ports in search of cargo. The Company tried by various means to stop them: furious lobbying in England merely led to the use of vessels sailing under a foreign flag;

attempting to intercept them at sea was risky and time consuming; and trying to impress upon local officials the importance of dealing only with the Company rarely met with success.

The most serious problem, however, lay with the Company's own servants, who knew exactly how the Company could turn a profit, and were keen to do so on their own account. The interlopers provided an ideal way for Company factors to conduct a private trade in parallel to the official one. Thomas Pitt (see page 97) started out as an interloper, and was rumoured to work hand-in-glove with all the Bengal factors. It took a monumental effort on the part of the Company to bring him to book, and his eventual £400 fine was no great deterrent. On his return to India he became Governor of Madras.

Interloping was a fact of Company daily life in the seventeenth century, but after the merger with their rival trading organisation in 1709, and with the increasing dominance of the Company in India, it became less of a problem than private trading.

PRIVATE AND COUNTRY TRADE

The Company would have preferred to pay its servants a set wage, and ban them from private trading, but no one would brave the risks of life in the East as a mere salaryman. The system which allowed ships' commanders to use cargo space for private trade was expanded to allow the Company's land-based traders to make substantial amounts of money without (at least in theory) jeopardising the Company's profits. The Company decided to condone the private trade that went on between eastern ports, but not, except where it was authorised, with Europe. The new rules were termed the 'country trade', and these could work to the Company's advantage when country traders pioneered new markets, such as those in Siam and Canton.

The distinctions between Company trade, private trade, country trade and interloping were frequently blurred, which makes it impossible to assess the value and profitability of the Company's commerce in isolation. In practice, the Company only drew the line at outright abuses by traders, such as the misuse of Company funds. The flexibility of these arrangements had the fortunate effect of creating a web of interconnected interests in the East, which held the burgeoning Company raj together more effectively than any directive from East India House.

ST HELENA

Far out in the South Atlantic, 1,700 miles north-west of Cape Town, and even further from Brazil to the west, lies the island of St Helena. It was discovered by the Portuguese in 1502 – a veritable Eden of gushing streams and dense forest guarded by looming cliffs, and perfectly placed on a south-east trade wind to provide a stopover for ships returning from the East; on the voyage out, ships tended to swing across the Atlantic towards Brazil to make use of the prevailing winds.

The Portuguese provided St Helena's first inhabitant – one Fernando López, who had made the mistake of allying himself against his countrymen in Goa. With characteristic forgiveness, the great Albuquerque merely chopped off his ears, nose, a hand and a thumb. López managed to stow away on a boat bound for home, wife and children. Consumed with sudden doubts about his likely reception, however, he jumped ship at St Helena, and lived there quite cheerfully, a curiosity to visiting ships' crews, cultivating pomegranates and palm trees, and keeping duck, hens and she-goats. He died in 1545, having lived on the island for nearly thirty years.

St Helena remained a valuable secret of the Portuguese until 1582, when the Elizabethan adventurer Fenton, and his second-in-command William Hawkins (see page 18), came upon it by chance.

Ten years later, another future Company officer, James Lancaster (see page 15), called in at the island on the First Voyage by Company ships to the East Indies. In 1603, Lancaster, in command of the East India Company's First Voyage, was returning home with the *Hector* and the *Dragon* when the *Dragon* lost its rudder in a storm off the Cape of Good Hope. Under Lancaster's cool command, the ships limped to St Helena for repairs. 'I live,' he wrote, 'at the devotion of the wind and seas'.

Finally, in 1659, Captain John Dutton, redirected from Pulo Run and charged with setting up a garrison and permanent fortifications, formally took possession of the island on behalf of the Company. The Company occupied St Helena, surviving insurrection by slaves, invasion by the Dutch, infestation by white ants and the incarceration of Napoleon, until 1834, when the Crown took it over to the great and lasting regret of the islanders.

In 1727, the Court of Directors decided to plant coffee on the island, and authorised their agent in Mocha to obtain

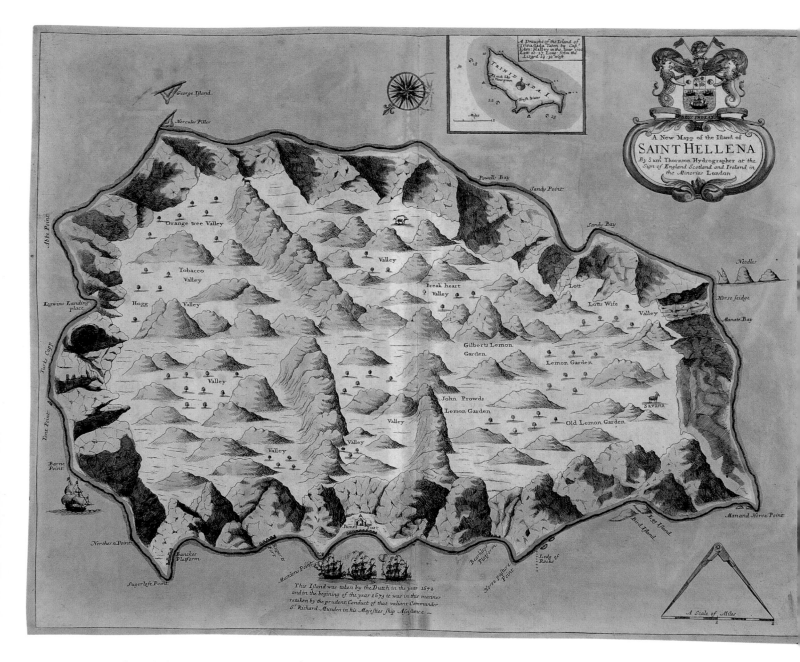

seed. Seeds from the main entrepôt, Bayt-al-Faquih (known endearingly as 'Beetlefuck' to the Company's servants) were shipped from Mocha on the *Houghton*, which arrived in St Helena on 10 February 1732.

A fledgling coffee industry developed, but it was only after Napoleon's arrival on the island in 1815 that St Helena's coffee received wider attention. The exiled Emperor was an inveterate coffee drinker, and after at first insisting that his coffee be brought from the French island of Réunion in the Indian Ocean, he sampled the local product and is said to have declared, 'The only good thing about St Helena is the coffee.' Maréchal Bertrand's memoirs recall the poignant moment when the Emperor, on his deathbed, asked for his last brew: 'Tears came to my eyes at the sight of this man, who had inspired such awe, who had given orders so proudly and positively, pleading now for a little spoonful of coffee, begging permission like a child, and not being given it, returning again and again to the same requests, always failing, and never getting angry.'

After Napoleon's death, St Helena coffee enjoyed a brief vogue among Parisians, but the highest accolade came at the Hyde Park Great Exhibition of 1851, where St Helena coffee was specially noted for its quality. Descendants of the same plants still flourish on the island, which today exports its crop worldwide at extremely high prices.

The Company narrowly missed having the distinction of incarcerating an emperor; instead, the Crown appointed a Governor – the despised Hudson Lowe – while Napoleon was on the island. After Napoleon's death, St Helena reverted to the Company until 1834, when the Crown finally took it over. It was a black day for the population. John Company had been a generous master, but under the Crown salaries were slashed, pensions reduced, subsidies cut, and the island reduced to a state of abject poverty from which it has never really recovered. Once the Suez Canal was opened, in 1869, there was simply no real reason to go there anymore.

OVERLAND ALTERNATIVES – THE MIDDLE EAST AND EGYPT

Considering the dangers and hardships of the sea voyage around the Cape of Good Hope, it is not surprising that many attempts to open up new routes to India were made over the years. In the nineteenth century, these efforts were lent further impetus by the increasing strategic and economic importance to the Crown of the Company's eastern possessions. In 1770, the only European merchants in Egypt were in Alexandria; by 1775, the Company had secured permission to sail up the Red Sea to Suez, and by the end of the decade had an official agent in Egypt, George Baldwin, who had sensed the coming strategic importance of Egypt for the security of India. As if to underline his point, Napoleon's invasion of Egypt sparked widespread concern in Company and government circles, and Nelson's crucial victory in the Battle of the Nile in 1798 was fought, not to liberate Egypt for its own sake, but to secure it as a vital stepping stone to India. The often invisible manoeuverings of the British to protect their eastern possession had begun.

For much of the eighteenth century it had been possible, through scarcely advisable, for travellers to the East to take the overland route from Alexandria to the Red Sea. Hugely uncomfortable, and often dangerous, it presented little competition to the sea route – which gives some idea of its hardships. More adventurous souls explored potential routes to Persia and thence to the Arabian Sea via, variously, Syria, Iraq, Russia and Turkey. Often these pioneers were in the service of the Company – sometimes sent as formal emissaries – and the written and visual records of their journeys provide compelling evidence of the lengths to which they went to maintain delicate commercial and diplomatic links with countries that lay on the way – if only theoretically – to India and the East. Indeed, for much of the eighteenth and nineteenth century English diplomatic appointments in these areas lay in the gift of the Government of India, and travellers from Persia to England would have first to go to India to secure the necessary permissions. These widespread contacts were of great assistance in securing Arab co-operation in the suppression of the slave trade.

In the 1820s, a lieutenant in the Company's Bombay Marine, Thomas Waghorn, conceived the idea that the existing, rather haphazard journey from Alexandria to Suez could, if improved, serve as a quick and efficient way of avoiding the sea voyage around the Cape. Steamships, unlike sailing ships, could make the passage of the Red Sea (which, because of winds, was only viable for three months in twelve) possible at all times of the year. Waghorn failed to attract significant support from the Company, but in 1829 got enough backing to put his idea into action when he personally delivered a message from London to the Governor in Bombay in forty days. The Company then sent other officers of the Bombay Marine to survey the notorious shallows of the Red Sea, one lamenting, 'But the scorching, roasting heat never leaves nor forsakes us!'

Waghorn's 'overland route' through Egypt had a rival – the 'Euphrates valley route' – and with characteristic thoroughness the Company examined the potential for that as well, commissioning a survey in 1829. This route held great hopes; it was over a thousand miles shorter, and would involve using steamships for river rather than sea passage. But the hopes literally foundered when the *Tigris*, one of the two steamships conveyed overland at enormous trouble and expense to the headwaters of the Euphrates, sank in a storm on the river in 1836, with the loss of 19 lives. Her sister ship, the *Euphrates,* continued to survey the river networks of Iraq, but Waghorn had regained the initiative, and in 1837 was appointed the Company's deputy agent in Egypt.

Indiamen and Steam Ships

In 1825, the Enterprise, *a 500-tonne paddle steamer moored at Calcutta; her paddles collapsed to allow the ship to sail when the winds suited. Built in Deptford by Gordon and Co, the ship was not a financial success but was an augury of the future. In 1829, the* Hugh Lindsay *arrived in Bombay from Suez, and within ten years P & O steamships were plying the route regularly. Steamships required coal, and, with characteristic pragmatism, the Company acquired Aden in 1839, and built the infrastructure needed for a*

coaling station; the coal itself made the long haul from Britain round the Cape. The voyage out to India was extended in 1845 to include Penang, Singapore and Hong Kong, and the next year Shanghai as well. The Lady Mary Wood, *a 600-tonne paddle steamer, arrived in Singapore, carrying mail which had been posted in London only 41 days earlier. The writing was on the wall for the magnificent sailing ships of the China trade, although they went out in a blaze of glory in their last incarnation as tea clippers.*

Looking towards home from the Company's Indian interests.

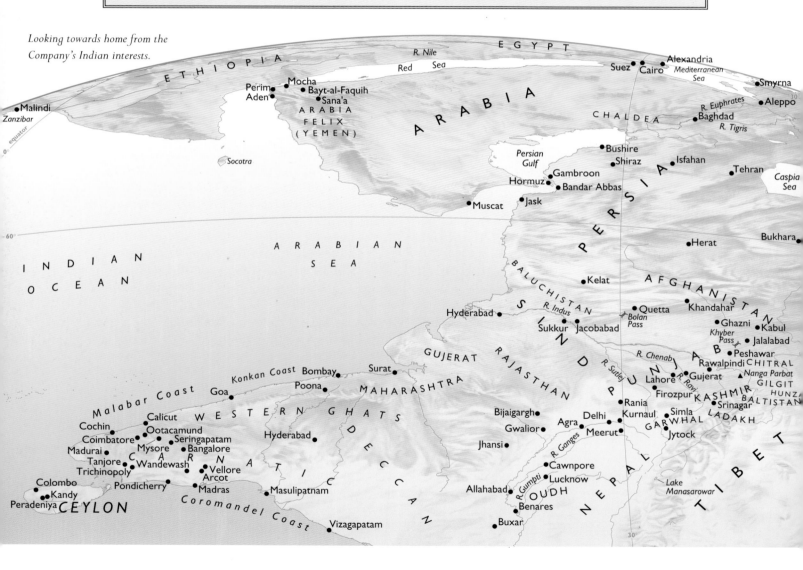

Waghorn established a series of rest-houses strung out on a well-policed route across the desert between Cairo and Suez, enabling travellers to make the previously perilous journey through bandit-ridden country with relative ease. Heliographs relayed information about the movement of ships, and passengers were able to enjoy the sights and antiquities around Cairo until the steamship arrived at Suez. Coaling stations were established at Aden and Perim, and the indefatigable Waghorn never ceased proselytising his vision; an exhausted William Makepeace Thackeray wrote, after meeting him in Cairo, 'He left Bombay yesterday morning, was seen in the Red Sea on Thursday, [and] is engaged to dine this afternoon in Regent's Park . . . '. Waghorn soon saw his precious route legitimised when the Company signed an agreement with the Peninsula and Oriental Steam Navigation Company (P & O) for the provision of a regular steam service from Suez to India. The era of 'Port Out Starboard Home' was born, awaiting only the opening of the Suez Canal in 1869 to make the Cape voyage virtually redundant.

The beach at Aden, a coaling station acquired by the Company in 1857, near the entrance to the Red Sea.

THE COMPANY
IN THE EAST

'War and trafique are incompatible.'

Sir Thomas Roe

The East India Company evolved in time into two quite different creatures: on the one hand there was the Company in India, where territorial, tax revenue and political interests had developed, although trade alone had initially been envisaged; and on the other there was the Company in the East where, bar the odd quirk like the Company's invasion of the Philippines and Java (see pages 87 and 89), territorial acquisition was kept to a minimum and trade assumed the priority that the Court of Directors in London desired. The Company's settlements in these areas were for the purpose of commerce only, and required some, but not much territory, and a small military presence for security – a division of the Indian army between all of them was considered sufficient.

Unlike in India, the Company further east was not a big player on the local political scene, nor did it suffer serious opposition from European rivals, apart from the Dutch in the early years. Towards the middle of the nineteenth century, the situation changed. Threats to the immensely important trade with China led to the Opium Wars, further 'treaty ports' were opened up for trade, and the Company's trading posts in Malaysia were merged into the Straits Settlements, under the administration of Calcutta and Singapore. Once the East India Company had ceased to be, the Crown's eastern interests in all these areas came more closely to resemble the Indian model.

The Company that ruled in India was dependent on its army; the Company that traded further east depended on the sea. The might of the Company and of the British navy came to be deployed in keeping the sea lanes open for trade against actual or potential enemies.

A view of Singapore, c. 1850. Stamford Raffles' creation was already a great commercial success.

CHAPTER VIII

SINGAPORE

DEFENCE OF THE SEA LANES

The encounter between a fleet of Indiamen under Commodore Dance and five French men o' war under Admiral Linois off the coast of Pulo Aor in the Spice Islands on 15 February 1804 became something of a cause célèbre in England. The heroic element lay in achieving a doughty victory against the odds and against Napoleon Bonaparte. The Company's presence in the area was a direct result of the decline of the Dutch East Indies Company, which had led to the opening up of the spice trade for the first time since the Company was founded some two centuries earlier. Buoyed by this success, the Company started to build up its presence in Penang in Malaysia – useful for maintaining a watchful eye on the China fleet. The eternally tempting prospect of a glittering free trade entrepôt in the East fuelled an ambitious expansion plan, which made Penang a fourth Presidency (see page 89), and put an obscure assistant secretary called Thomas Stamford Raffles on the launch pad of a career that was to propel him to fame as the founder of Singapore (see page 91).

The Straits of Malacca sit at the intersection of the different monsoon cycles of the Indian Ocean and the South China Sea, and to sailors marked the entrance to Far Eastern waters. They also marked the start of the influence of the region's largest power, China: Chinese communities,

Company Factories in the East

Name	Modern location	Established	Comments
Bantam (Djakarta)	Java	1602	Expelled by the Dutch, 1682
Bencoolen (region)	Sumatra	1603	New lease of life in 1685
Macassar	Sulawesi	1610	Short-lived
Pulo Run	Banda Islands	1616	Defeated by Dutch, 1620
Ayutthaya	Thailand	1612	Short-lived
Patani	Thailand	1612	Short-lived
Amboyna	Spice Islands	1620	Massacred by Dutch, 1623
Ternate	Spice Islands	1620	Abandoned after pressure from Dutch
Banda Island	Banda Islands	1620	Abandoned after pressure from Dutch
	Cambodia	1654	Short-lived
Tonking	Vietnam	1672	Abandoned, 1697
Patani	Thailand	1675	Short-lived. Trouble with interlopers
Ayutthaya	Thailand	1675	Short-lived. Trouble with interlopers
Bencoolen	Sumatra	1685	Ceded by treaty with Dutch, 1824
Amoy	China	1676	Superseded by Canton
Ningpo	China	1676	Superseded by Canton
Pulo Condore	Vietnam	1703	Massacred by Bugis, 1706
Canton	China	1699	Temporary facilities
Manila	Philippines	1762	Taken from Spain, then returned
Penang	Malaysia	1786	New settlement
Malacca	Malaysia	1795	Captured from Dutch, returned, then taken back in return for Bencoolen, 1824
Singapore	Singapore	1819	New settlement

(Penang, Malacca and Singapore became the Straits Settlements in 1826, under the administration of Calcutta and Singapore.)

sailors, pirates and junks proliferated from there onwards, and the English came to rely on the Chinese as middlemen in their commercial dealings. China itself provided the most significant trade for the Company, but other factories and settlements grew up with varying degrees of success.

When the Company's factories in the East failed, they did so because of massacres, rival trade, sickness, superfluousness, interlopers, pirates, politics or poverty.

Given Ceylon's proximity to India and its wealth of spices, it is surprising that the Company did not cast a more covetous eye on the island, which had been litorally occupied by the Portuguese and the Dutch since the start of the colonial era. When eventually the English did make their move, in 1795, they acted in the name of the Crown, not the Company – as they did later, when they ousted the remaining Kandyan Kings from the interior. The English Governors of the island were Crown servants, even though, like so much in eastern affairs, the Company and the Crown seemed interchangeable.

FACTORY LIFE

The 'factory', the standard Company trading post in the East Indies until the Company's role became territorial in India, was a combination of a warehouse and an Oxbridge college. Its *raison d'être* was to enable merchants (or 'factors') to buy goods at whatever time of year the price was lowest, and store them against the arrival of one of their ships. Usually grouped around a courtyard, or surrounded by a stockade, the warehouse and the dining room provided both work and pleasure – the latter was a mess-hall in which all the Company's factors would eat, the chief factor at the head and the others arranged in strict hierarchy. Prayers were said each morning, and the English flag hoisted every Sunday. Bedrooms above were usually fairly spartan, again ranked by seniority.

There might be as few as eight men in a factory, with only each other for company for years on end. There was little to do once the day-trips around the area had been exhausted; some experimented with gardening, others lapsed into excessive drinking. Tropical diseases, little understood, frequently laid waste the factory: 'All our servants are sick and dead, and at this moment there is not a cook to get victuals ready for those that sit at the Company's Table . . . we have no living to bury the dead.' Fort Marlborough (Bencoolen) in Sumatra, the unfortunate location of this ghastly scene in

1685, had outlying posts spread over three hundred miles of coast, a small garrison and a complement of some thirty Company servants – factors, warehousemen, bookeepers and secretaries – as well as writers, five surgeons to keep them healthy, and a chaplain to bury them when the surgeons failed. The factory was notably liberal in its attitude to relationships between the men and local women, but 'Bencoolen fever' was the frequent result.

Bencoolen's other distinction was that under the Company it saw the first tentative steps towards the plantation system that was to dominate much of the British Empire. These pepper plantations were set up by private traders or retired Company servants. Worked by slave labour until Raffles banned it, 'debt slaves' – locals offered a lump sum to be repaid by work – then took over. The ceding of the Bencoolen factory and allied settlements to the Dutch in return for Malacca saw the end of this experiment.

Outside the Company's sphere of activities were the adventurers, the most famous of whom, 'the White Rajah of Sarawak', James Brooke, founded an independent ruling dynasty. Others were less successful; the port of Mergui on the coast of Siam was taken over by a motley population of seamen, interlopers and men dismissed from the Company's service. Most were massacred by the Siamese in 1687.

SOME MISTAKES

The earliest of the Company's trading posts and its last forlorn hope against the might of the Dutch in the Spice Islands, the Bantam factory, was abandoned under pressure from the Dutch in 1682. It was a particularly pestilential post, being sited by mosquito-infested marshes and cursed with a vile, sweltering climate. The great Company ship, the *Trades' Increase,* ended its life as a burnt-out hulk on the mudflats, serving as a temporary hospital for the sick of the English factory, which was nearly all of them.

At the instigation of the Crown, the Company took possession of Manila in the Philippines from 1762 for a period of eighteen months. Captured by surprise from the Spanish as a favour to the Government, which had occasionally helped them out in India, the Company had no idea what to do with its sudden acquisition; squabbles broke out in the Manila Council, and the troops mutinied. Luckily, the Treaty of Paris handed the Philippines back to the Spanish, and the Company withdrew, if not gracefully, then at least gratefully.

PENANG

Francis Light, a captain in the Bombay Marine, secured the island of Penang for the Company from the Sultan of Kedah in 1786, making it the Company's first territorial acquisition east of India. It took only a hundred and fifty men to garrison the new settlement, a force which was not increased for twenty years. It quickly became the haunt of the private trader, as it was designated a free port and thus outside the monopoly of the Company. Although by 1805 Prince of Wales Island (its official new title) had grown sufficiently to be deemed a fourth Presidency, and given its own Governor, it never achieved anything like the status of its Indian counterparts. It had been hoped to use it as a naval base and shipyard, but lack of suitable local timber made this impossible. With the title of Presidency came the full majesty of English law, which the settlement was allowed to administer from 1808. The church followed: St George's was completed in 1819, and designed, in true Company style, not by an architect but by Captain Robert Smith of the Bengal Engineers.

Georgetown, the capital of the settlement, in common with the Company's other eastern settlements, was divided into commercial and segregated residential quarters. This practice, which might seem at first glance to be based on racial prejudice, was in fact based on a system inherited from Malay kings in Malacca.

Prince of Wales Island had been parcelled out by Francis Light to early colonists, mainly private traders, but the Company later refused to grant long leases, and many plantations fell vacant. The leading landowner, David Brown, lived in some style at Glugor House surrounded by his nutmeg and clove plantations; he had bought up the few remaining properties on perpetual lease as they came up for sale. His spices thrived, and eventually other landowners followed suit, until half the island was covered with cloves and nutmeg.

JAVA

In order to keep out Napoleon, who had overrun Holland and taken control of all Dutch overseas possessions, the Company mounted a full-scale invasion of the island of Java in 1611, with eighty-one ships and nine thousand men. The

Glugor House, the elegant estate of David Brown on Penang.

invasion was the brainchild of Stamford Raffles, who through hard work and 'insatiable' ambition had risen through the ranks from a clerkship at East India House at the age of fourteen to become Chief Secretary of Malacca in 1807, at the age of twenty-five. There he caught the eye of Lord Minto, the Governor General, whose personal agent he became, and together they planned the invasion, which went remarkably smoothly. Javanese princes were persuaded that to be relieved from the French yoke was a good thing, and after a short fight opposing Dutch troops who had been forced to wear French army hats took them off and stamped on them.

By his thirtieth birthday Raffles had become Lieutenant Governor of over five million people, master of all the Dutch East Indies, and answerable only to Minto. The only fly in his ointment was that the conclusion of a treaty ending the war in Europe would probably mean that he would have to give it all back again. His rule was a benevolent one, though the presence of so many Company soldiers meant that most administrative posts were taken by senior army men. General Rollo Gillespie surprised the Dutch by purchasing a harem of slave-girls, 'something very unusual for an Englishman'. Gillespie resented Raffles' position, and reported him to the new Governor General, Lord Moira (later Lord Hastings), on charges of corruption. As a result, Raffles was removed in 1815, and shortly after that the island returned to Dutch control. Raffles' imperial appetite had been whetted, however, and he soon returned to the fray, first in Bencoolen then again in Malacca.

SINGAPORE

Singapore, unlike Hong Kong, was a creation of the East India Company. Or, more correctly, the Company in the form of Moira, now Lord Hastings, allowed itself to be persuaded by Raffles, now Governor of Bencoolen, that it needed a secure base at the head of the strategically vital Straits of Malacca. Raffles' case was reinforced by the activities of the Dutch, who had been given back Malacca itself but seemed bent on excluding English ships from the area. Raffles had probably provoked the Dutch hostility, but was in any case charged by Hastings to find a suitable place for a

Sir Stamford Raffles. From Company clerk in London to Governor of Java and founder of Singapore.

settlement. With two cruisers and a hundred sailors of the Bombay Marine, and three hundred and forty Bengal sepoys aboard, he selected Sinhapura, a small island at the very tip of the Malay peninsula. A deal was quickly struck with the Sultan of Johore, and the Union Jack hoisted. The military presence ensured that the Dutch would not interfere. Within days, Malays and Chinese had started to arrive from Malacca, and by the time the Company in London heard of their latest eastern acquisition, the island had a population of five thousand.

The foundation of Singapore is thus generally credited to Raffles, although in fact he only signed a treaty allowing the establishment of a Company trading post; it was his successor, John Crawfurd, who actually signed the secession treaty granting sovereignty. Singapore was, however, the product of Raffles' vision and decision, and although the Directors grumbled, he was loyally supported by Hastings. It did not help him personally; in 1824, he returned to London in ill-health, impoverished and mourning the death of three of his four children. Far from rewarding his thirty years of service, the Directors, with their usual parsimony, demanded £22,000 they claimed that he owed them. Raffles died shortly after, and his widow paid the Company £10,000 to settle the matter. By 1857, it was estimated that the total trade of Singapore had reached £10,000,000.

FORTUNES

> **LOOT**, *s. & v. Plunder; Hind. lut....Skt.lotra*
> *Hobson-Jobson*

COMPANY MEN

John Mowbray was typical of the merchants working out of Bengal in the late eighteenth century. His partner, Thomas Graham, was the Company's Resident in Benares, which opened significant opportunities for country trade (see page 79). Private trade of this kind naturally led to frequent conflicts of interest: how would one choose between either supporting the interests of the Company or granting a favour at the expense of the Company which allowed private profit? Most of the day-to-day business was conducted through an Indian agent known as a banian (in the north) or a dubash (in the south). Although nominally acting on behalf of their masters, they, too, were able to trade on their own account, and many became rich as a result. The commercial advantage that the Company gained through its territorial expansion made many individuals, Company servants or otherwise, considerable fortunes; the wealth of many of today's great Indian business dynasties began in this way, as well as that of distinguished families such as the Tagores in Bengal.

WILLIAM FULLERTON

Dr William Fullerton's time in the Company's service, although by no means typical, shows the tortuous and often dangerous trajectory a career in India could take. Joining the Company in 1744, he was appointed as a second surgeon in Calcutta in 1751, and after the crisis of the Black Hole, which he survived, he was elected mayor. He took to speculating in the saltpetre trade, the control of which had become one of the perks of the Company's new power in Bengal. He was more interested in India than many of his contemporaries, mastered several Indian languages, received Indian friends, probably had a couple of Indian mistresses, and was a keen patron of the arts, with a partic-

ular interest in the holy men of India. He was also employed as an interpreter for the enquiry into the Patna Massacre of which he was sole survivor, and, as a result, was attacked by the English for 'native intrigue'.

Fullerton's career, although controversial, was not tainted by the charge of corruption; the same could not be said of many of his contemporaries in India.

WILLIAM FRASER

In 1979, the cellars of a Scottish house revealed a hidden treasure: the complete correspondence from India of the Fraser family, as well as a wealth of unique paintings of the Company School.

The Company provided a useful career opportunity for scions of the impoverished landowners of Scotland and Ireland, many of whom had been left behind by the newly created wealth of the industrial revolution. Not all took the risk that Edward Fraser did in allowing his entire succession of five sons to go to India (four in the Company's service, the fifth as a Calcutta merchant) but in other ways the Fraser family was typical of a Scots landowning family seeking ways to boost the dwindling income derived from their estate. The first essential for anyone seeking employment with the Company was a connection with a Director: Charles Grant did the honours, and recommended William, the second son, for the position of writer in Bengal, where he won the Gold Medal at the Company's training college at Fort William in Calcutta. An able linguist, he seemed well adapted to India life, even adopting a hybrid Anglo-Indian look, which had fallen out of fashion except in elaborately posed fantasy portraits.

Fraser was appointed assistant to the Resident at Delhi, where he diligently implemented the Company's settlement policy, practised moderation in food and drink, and only hunted tigers from the relative safety of an elephant's back, on his father's advice. He seemed 'half Asiatick in his habits', grew a beard and became a vegetarian, attracting the comment that he was 'as much Hindoo as Christian' from the disapproving memsahib of his Commander-in-Chief, whilst in turn complaining that his compatriots had 'no rational conversation'. Through supplementing his

John Mowbray in conference with his banian, 1790. A cluttered desk conceals a successful commercial brain.

Much admired by William Fraser, the Nepalese Ghurkhas carried their trademark kukri with its lethal 14-inch curved blade.

good income with horse-breeding on the farm of a friend, Colonel James Skinner, and trading in partnership with the Nawab of Firozpur, he was able in 1811 to send his father £2,000 to prop up the family fortunes. Although confiding to his brother that he had a bibi and children in Rania, north of Delhi, he maintained the pretence to the rest of his family that he lived a chaste bachelor life, writing home, 'It is enough for me to reflect how many valuable women are to be had in Britain, to hinder me from risking the charms of a hundred or more in India. So I must wait until I go home & then it will be too late' (William Fraser, *Fraser Papers*, Bundle 439, National Register of Archives, Scotland).

Fraser was offered the position of second-in-command in Colonel Skinner's irregular troop of cavalry, Skinner's Horse, causing a friend to comment 'whenever there is a war anywhere, he throws up his judicial functions and goes to it'. He was appointed Political Agent in the war with Nepal, and shortly afterwards Commissioner of Garwhal, where he formed his own irregular cavalry using renegade Ghurkhas, whose strength and endurance he valued highly, as well as men from other mountain tribes. He was joined by his eldest brother James, whom he had last seen in Scotland some sixteen years previously, and James was proud of the transformation that his now celebrated brother had undergone. At the head of a motley force of over a thousand men, William toured his new territory, asserting British supremacy over Ghurkha insurgents. James's paintings of this tour eventually formed a fine series of aquatints (opposite), published in London as *Views of the Himala Mountains*, and these were followed later by a series of Calcutta scenes.

William continued to combine a political and military life, finding time to commission paintings by local Delhi artists of dancing girls, his bibi, his irregulars, and his loyal orderly, Ummee Chund, who was to save him from assassi-

nation in 1819. These early examples of 'Company' paintings focus for the first time on portrait subjects, rather than natural history or architecture. William also collected oriental manuscripts, and it is reasonably certain that the so-called Emperor's (or Kevorkian) Album that forms the centrepiece of the New York Metropolitan Museum's oriental collection was William's; it was bought by an American tourist in a Scottish antique shop for £100 in 1929.

Ummee Chund was unfortunately not on hand to prevent William Fraser's death at the hands of an assassin on the streets of Delhi in 1835. The man behind the killing was caught and hanged – the eldest son of William's old horse-

A 1760 portrait of a European, probably Dr William Fullerton, seated Indian-style with a hookah.

The Ridge and Fort of Jytock. A view of the Himala Mountains painted by James Fraser whilst on tour with his brother William.

dealing partner, the Nawab of Firozpur, embittered by the settlement of a family dispute enforced in his official capacity by William.

A final touch to this extraordinary and exotic life was discovered on William's death, when it was found that he had secretly in his possession the diaries of William Moorcroft (see page 10). Moorcroft had disappeared mysteriously on a trip to Bukhara, supposedly in search of horses, but it was rumoured that he had been on an espionage mission in the high mountain territories which were to become the backdrop for the 'Great Game', the struggle between the imperial interests of Russia and Britain immortalised by Kipling. Fraser's possession of Moorcroft's diary has never been satisfactorily explained.

Of Edward Fraser's five sons, two died in Delhi, one in Calcutta, one in St Helena, and only James made it back to the family's estate at Moniack, near Inverness. He married a cousin, Jane Tytler, a local girl who failed to understand the ties that bind, and with no apology stopped the visits of the half-caste children of James Skinner to the house.

GIFTS, GRATUITIES AND GREED

Clive once famously declared himself 'astonished at my own moderation', but even today it is possible to be astonished at his wealth. When he arrived in England in 1760 he had with him £230,000 in Dutch bills, £41,000 in bills on the Company, £30,000 in diamonds, £7,000 in bills on a Company Director, and £5,000 in bills on the Company in Bombay. A tidy sum now, but then, stupendous.

Lesser mortals fared spectacularly well, too; even subalterns in Clive's army had received £5,000 after Plassey. (Later Clive was to declare rather grandly that for a subaltern to make a fortune in India was 'averse to those Duties of Subordination which are Inseparable from the Life of a Soldier'.)

The fact that the Bengal ruler Mir Jafar was replaced by Mir Kasim led to substantial 'gifts', then still more when Mir Jafar replaced him in turn. Mir Jafar's death in 1765 led to a final round of gifts from the incoming Nawab of some £112,000. Between 1757 and 1765, an estimated total of

Clive meeting Mir Jafar in a suitably suppliant mood after the Battle of Plassey in 1757.

£2,000,000 was paid out in the form of gifts by various Nawabs in this game of musical thrones, and if further payments could not be extracted, it was because there was precious little left; the entire revenue of Bengal at this time was about £2,500,000 a year.

Gifts from grateful rulers was one way of making money; less direct, but equally effective, was to have the right position in the Company's service. James Johnston, Bengal councillor, retired with £300,000; Richard Smith, Commander-in-Chief, £250,000; Sir Thomas Rombold, Resident at Patna, £200,000; Francis Sykes, Resident at Murshibad, similar; Richard Barlow, Bengal councillor, £400,000. Even 'beardless boys' in the Company's service in Lucknow were known to reject 'with indignation gratuities of 3,000 and 5,000 rupees . . . clerks in office, clamouring for principalities, threatening those who hes-

itated to gratify their want with vengeance of patronage' (Warren Hastings, letter).

The creaming off of revenues, kickbacks on the granting of contracts or monopolies, and privileged private trading were the standard ruses, usually at the expense of the Company. It must have seemed to those at home that there was indeed a 'pagoda tree' in India from which gold coins (pagodas) could be shaken. There were different attitudes to corruption in those times, as well as an ever-present sense of the risks involved in being in India; half of those who went out in the eighteenth century never returned.

It should also be remembered that at the time it was standard practice for pay to be supplemented by prize money in the British army and Royal Navy, shared out according to rank. The potential to make money was one of the principal motivating forces for taking the risks that action implied,

Precious Stones

The opulence of the Moghul Court and the princely states was legendary, and their dazzling jewels and semi-precious stones attracted a great deal of attention. Until Brazilian mines opened in the 1860s, India was the only source of the world's diamonds. The Company had sent a jeweller, Hugh Greete, to buy diamonds for the Moghuls, but he had been caught purloining the best and was sent back in disgrace in 1618. The famous Pitt diamond, foundation of a political dynasty, was sought, and bought by Thomas Pitt, Governor of Madras, as a means of turning the fortune he had made in India into readily transportable capital; he bought the 400-carat gem from a dealer in Madras for £24,000 and sold it in Europe fifteen years later to the Regent of France for £135,000.

The Koh-i-nor (above), now part of the British crown jewels, was confiscated at the conclusion of the Sikh War; John Lawrence, with admirable otherworldliness, tucked it into a waistcoat pocket, and promptly forgot about it. His valet saved his subsequent embarrassment when Queen Victoria enquired about it, recalling that he had seen a piece of glass in his master's pocket. The Company had wanted to keep the diamond to pay for the war, but the Governor General, Lord Dalhousie, had promised that it would 'find its final and fitting resting place in the crown of Britain'.

The association of India with diamonds, and the superstition that goes with them, finds its strongest literary expression in Wilkie Collins'

The Moonstone, in which shadowy Brahmins commit murder in a Yorkshire country house to retrieve a yellow diamond that had been stolen from a Hindu shrine.

The technique of cutting and faceting stones, which is now almost universal, was not known in India in the Company's time. Gems (the Moghul spoon below is of gold, studded with rubies) were rather crudely rounded off before being mounted for turbans, rings and necklaces. What they lacked in brilliance they made up for in size. Hobson-Jobson notes laconically, concerning the cutting of the Koh-i-nor, 'In 1850-51, before being shown at the Great Exhibition in Hyde Park, it went through a process of cutting which, for reasons unintelligible to ordinary mortals, reduced its weight from 186 $\frac{1}{16}$ carats to 106 $\frac{1}{16}$.' Surat, the scene of the East India Company's first activities in India, is now the centre of the world diamond-cutting industry.

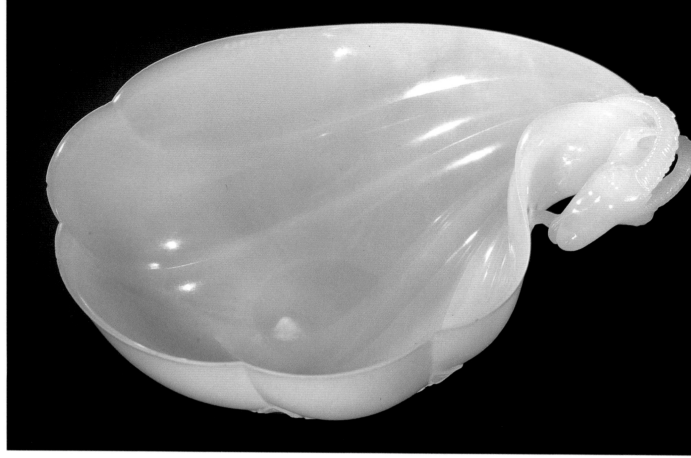

The Emperor Shah Jehan's wine cup, exquisitely carved from nephrite jade.

and other opportunities for trading or receiving kickbacks from contracts were seen as the normal perquisites of a life on active service. The Indian army was no different in this respect, and, given that the successes in Bengal were first and foremost military in origin, it is perhaps understandable that the bounty should have been shared in the traditional way.

The loss of the American colonies led to a national heart-searching, and corrupt practices which had been tolerated on a wave of successes were suddenly considered symptoms of something rotten in the state. Administration in the regular British army was reformed, and after Pitt's India Act in 1784, the Indian army's new Commander-in-Chief, Lord Cornwallis, set the tone by foregoing a £6,000 annual salary to which he was perfectly entitled. The heady, rapacious days of Clive were giving way to an era of duty, service and the high moral ground. Home's painting of Cornwallis receiving the Mysore hostages (page 151) embodies this new zeitgeist, depicting the General as a man of generous, civilised values dispensing justice tempered with mercy to the wily oriental. Cornwallis himself was sufficiently wily to leave the introduction of far-reaching and controversial army reforms until he was safely on the boat home.

WAR ON CORRUPTION

Lord North's Regulating Act was passed in 1773 – prompting, by a loophole in the wording, the Boston Tea Party, an altogether more picturesque swipe at the Company (see page 144). The Act was an attempt to reimpose some order on the Company's behaviour in India, particularly to control those Company servants who had amassed, or were in the process of amassing, huge fortunes on the back of the Company at the expense of the Indian kingdoms they were milking. Principal among the new rules was an end to the private trade of Company servants on their own account. However, although this stamped out one abuse, it merely gave rise to others – the Company might find itself overcharged for labour or materials in a construction project; as late as 1781, a Colonel Hannay, after three years as revenue collector for three districts in Oudh, retired with a fortune of £300,000.

The problems were to some extent caused by Clive himself, who had set a precedent for the receipt of gifts when he placed Mir Jafar on the throne of Bengal after the 'Battle' of Plassey. Clive managed to justify his present of £234,000 as unsolicited, therefore uncorrupt. As a fall-back position, he outlined to parliament the temptations that had faced him – rooms full of gold and jewels – so that 'I stand astonished at my own moderation'. Doublespeak came naturally to Clive, whose naked ambition was cloaked in an enormous sense of his own destiny. He sought a seat in the House of Lords (and had to be content with a mere Irish peerage); he fought for, and won, seats in parliament not only for himself but his cronies (family and placemen); he set himself up in great style on country estates from Shropshire to Surrey, and had a luxurious house in Berkeley Square.

All this, allied to the largest individual fortune in England, made Clive a force to be reckoned with, but he had not reckoned with the resistance of the Establishment, nor the vicious politicking within the Company, his supposed area of expertise. Far from the grateful nation allowing Clive of India to be borne to high office on a wave of goodwill, Clive found himself manoeuvering and lobbying with the rest of them. It was a bad time for both the nation and the Company. George III was keen to flex his muscles, Pitt was on the wane, and there was no clear-cut mandate for either Tory or Whig. The Company had elected the cautious Lawrence Sulivan as chairman – one of the few old India hands to reach that position – who was implacably opposed to the aggrandising ideas of Clive.

On top of all this came the disastrous famine in Bengal of 1769-70. Nearly half the population (some three million people) died, and land revenues plummeted. Clive's achievements came under attack on two fronts: first, he had promised that the revenues from Bengal would finance the Company's expansionist operations in India, but in fact the Company found itself sliding rapidly into debt; second, the famine exposed the greed and self-interest of the Nabobs, who, as far as public perception in England was concerned, had raped Bengal, then cast her out to die. While the first was certainly true, the second charge ignored Indian history – famines occurred on an all-too-regular basis, whoever was in power. Clive was called to account for himself to parliament and, as a result of some behind-the-scenes lobbying by Sulivan, particular attention was paid to the gloriously-titled 'black jagir', Clive's share of the diwani which guaranteed him an income of £27,000 a year for life. He had secured this income from Mir Jafar, who in turn had secured it on revenues that he was to receive from the Company for the lease of certain lands. In effect, Clive was the Company's landlord, an arrangement to which the Company had initially agreed but came to rue. Clive himself attached disproportionate importance to the diwani: substantial as it was, its withdrawal would not ruin him, as he seemed to think ('my future power, my future grandeur, all depend upon the receipt of the jagir money'). Perhaps for him the diwani was a symbolic validation of his actions, annually reiterated. In any case, a deal was struck with the Company whereby he was to keep the revenue for ten years or his lifetime, whichever was the shorter. He committed suicide shortly after the expiry of this term, in 1775.

Whatever Clive's problems, they were insignificant compared to those of the Company, which, owing to the cash-flow crisis caused by the famine, needed to borrow a million pounds. Parliament seized the opportunity to exert pressure on the Company in return for the loan, and the Regulating Act was passed. It was a poor piece of legislation, managing to be both too little too late and too much too soon. The worst corruption was already over – the level of gift-giving had fallen from an estimated £2,000,000 between 1757 and 1765 to paltry levels thereafter. But, because of the political fallout of the corruption scandals, parliament imposed an almost unworkable structure for the future governance of India. The unfortunate man who had to try to make sense of it all was Warren Hastings, a Company official with many years service in India and an unimpeacheable record; but impeached he finally was.

Hastings was appointed Governor General, working out of the now senior Calcutta Presidency. He chaired, and had casting vote in a Council of four, appointed by the Company and parliament as a check on the Governor General, while the Supreme Court in India had new powers, effectively giving it the status of final arbiter in the land.

He had an old friend, Elijah Impey, in the Supreme Court, and could more-or-less rely on two of his fellow councillors, but the third, Philip Francis, was determined from the outset to bring about Hastings' downfall. No intrigue was too much for Francis, who allied himself to a known forger to gain false depositions against Hastings, was constantly engaged in secret sniping correspondence with the Directors back home, and undermined Hastings in public and in private to Coote, his Commander-in-Chief, and to the other councillors. At the same time the Mahrattas were threatening war, and Hyder Ali in the south declared it. Under these enormous pressures Hastings behaved with relative decency (his main breach being the somewhat summary hanging of the forger), but he finally decided to force Francis to challenge him to a duel through a calculated

insult. The ensuing duel ended with Hastings unscathed and Francis, although only slightly wounded, politically crippled. But Hastings emerged strangely altered: whereas before he had seemed by and large above the kind of corrupt and arbitrary behaviour Francis was constantly accusing him of, as soon as Francis was off the scene he began to behave, uncharacteristically, with an impetuous lack of judgement, exposing himself to the sort of criticism that he had done so well to parry in more difficult times. It was evident that both he and the Company had had enough, and Hastings returned to England in 1778 for what he thought would be an honoured and honourable retirement.

Francis, however, defeated in India, resumed his bitter personal campaign against Hastings back in England. Aided by the formidable oratorical skills of Edmund Burke (an opposition backbencher trying to make his political mark), and with the tacit backing (for political reasons of his own) of Pitt the Younger, Francis succeeded in engineering impeachment proceedings. The trial in Westminster Hall — played before the fashionable in the manner of a dramatic performance, with seats for sale and even two royal boxes — stretched over eight years, nearly bankrupted Hastings, but brought a full acquittal.

It was a trial that undermined the reputation of the parliamentary process itself. Hastings emerges from history relatively unscathed. His rule in India less self-interested than most, his legacy to the next Governor General, Lord Cornwallis, considerably less corrupt than when he received it. In his passion for oriental culture and scholarship and his firm belief that as far as possible Indian laws and customs should be studied and respected, he was a man ahead of his time. As he said during his trial: 'I gave you all; and you have rewarded me with confiscation, disgrace and a life of impeachment.'

The trial of Warren Hastings played to capacity crowds in Westminster Hall.

EAST MEETS WEST

'It was in the eighteenth century that Indian History started.'

W C Sellar and R J Yeatman, *1066 and All That*

The most mysterious and impenetrable of the social arrangements which Europeans encountered in India was the zenana, the quarters where the many wives of wealthy or aristocratic men were hidden from other men's view – and temptation. Purdah, literally 'a curtain', was not the sole preserve of either Muslim or Hindu but espoused by both religions. It was virtually impossible for European men to penetrate the zenana, but as time went on their womenfolk – or at least those with curiosity and knowledge of the language – felt quite at ease visiting Indian women there. Far from being suppressed and dull, the women of the zenana were often found to be refined, witty, and sharp observers of human foibles. Mrs Fanny Parks, who lived in India in the early nineteenth century and who would abandon her long-suffering husband, a Company official in Allahabad, to go on adventures of her own devising, thought the women of the zenana 'remarkably graceful' while European ladies were 'as stiff as a lobster in its shell'. Of Mrs Parks, Lord Auckland wrote: 'She has a husband who goes mad in the cold season, so she says it is her duty to herself to leave him and travel about.'

Pretty and irrepressible, Mrs Parks is one of the most appealing of the English women chroniclers of the Indian scene: she learnt Persian, Hindi and the sitar, loved Indian cookery, chess and even tried opium, reporting that she felt extremely well 'and talked incessantly'. With typical candour she watched a hook-swinging ceremony: 'I was greatly disgusted, but greatly fascinated.' Her open nature made her easy company: she befriended the ex-queen of Gwalior, and amused her Court with demonstrations of how to ride side-saddle. She wrote a book about her experiences, with the appealing title *Wanderings of a Pilgrim in Search of the Picturesque* (London 1850, repr. 1975).

An Indian courtesan with her attendant. Graceful and refined, courtesans could present a startling contrast to the memsahib.

CHAPTER X

Nob Kitschen's nautch party in Patna, 1825. A far cry from the stiff-upper-lip image of the British raj.

TEMPTATION AND THE BIBI

The subcontinent was not short of temptations for Englishmen who were far from home and hearth, and thrown into a sensual, exotic and alien world. John MacDonald (*Memoirs of an 18th Century Footman*, Century, 1985) describes a visit to a princely court: 'The Prince went out; and, soon after, came two fine black girls, the Princes' slaves, dressed in the Moorish manner; they had rings on their fingers, ears and toes, and bangles on their arms; their breasts were covered with various ornaments . . . they had neither shift nor stockings, but a thin silk gauze for petticoat . . . The finest dressed one entered first; put her two hands to her forehead then her breasts, and with her two hands touched the Colonel's foot: this is called the grand salaam. In like manner the other paid her compliments to Mr Wood.' Then, with the diplomatic lightness of touch that must have made him valued as a steward, he adds: 'After the compliments were over, I was going. My Master said: "John, if I don't come on board tonight I shall in the morning." On another occasion the gentlemen manage to peep at the ladies in the zenana of a local muslim. One gentleman said, "They are pretty"; another said, "They are richly dressed"; "I wish we had them here," said another.'

European expansion into Asia 'was not only a matter of "Christianity and commerce"; it was also a matter of copulation and concubinage,' (Ronald Hyam, *Empire and Sexuality,* MUP, 1991). The patronage of courtesans was commonplace, and they were highly praised by their clientele. 'They understand in perfection all the arts and wiles of love, are capable of gratifying any tastes, and in face and figure they are unsurpassed by any women in the world' (Captain Edward Sellon, *In India* 1834-44). A noted libertine, the writer mentions the women of Europe, 'but never, never did they bear comparison with those salacious succulent houris of the far East.'

The practice of keeping a bibi — an Indian mistress or wife — was well established at all levels of the Company by the eighteenth century. The bibi was often called the 'sleeping dictionary', as bibis were the most enjoyable way for Company men to learn a language. A scarcity of European women, the likelihood of spending years in India, and, no doubt, an all-too intimate acquaintance with the mortality statistics, combined to make the custom widely accepted. Although estimates vary, in the early eighteenth century as many as ninety per cent of marriages may have been with Indian or Anglo-Indian women, and were frequently happy: 'I have observed that those who have lived with a native woman for any length of time never marry a European . . . so amusingly playful, so anxious to oblige and please, that a person after being accustomed to their society shrinks from the idea of encountering the whims or yielding to the fancies of an Englishwoman' (S Sneade Brown, *Home letters written from India* 1828-41, London 1878).

Many bachelor bungalows had a bibikhana built behind them for the discreet accommodation of the bibi. For some, however, discretion was of no consequence: Sir David Ochterlony, Resident of Delhi, regularly rode around the city followed by his thirteen wives on a elephant each, and was thoroughly 'Brahminised' in his dress and tastes. He eventually conquered Nepal, and his memorial in Calcutta combines Greek, Egyptian and Islamic themes as a tribute to his multiculturalism.

The growth of the Anglo-Indian population (a term only recently used for people of mixed blood; it was originally used for those English born and raised in India) led to an awkward confusion of the ruler and the ruled which was never resolved. Initially, intermarriage was encouraged, with children receiving Company christening presents, on the basis that such unions would provide soldiers in the years to come. In 1791, a new edict excluded the Anglo-Indians from the Company's military and civil service; subsequently Governor Wellesley banned them from Government House entertainment, and by 1835 intermarriage itself was forbidden. Although Anglo-Indians managed to carve out niches for themselves — in the management echelons of the nascent Indian Railways, for example — there was no question of social parity with the Europeans.

Sir David Ochterlony watching nautch dancers at the Residency in Delhi. His dour Scots ancestors look on.

Rinaldi captures the tenderness of Major William Palmer's unorthodox domesticity: Delhi wife on his right, Lucknow wife on his left.

By the mid-nineteenth century, with the increasing presence of the memsahib, the missionary and the regular P & O steamer, few excuses remained for the keeping of a bibi, except perhaps in the remoter plantations (though even there, 'proper' wives were known to take umbrage when they discovered their husband with an extensive local family). One of the reasons why the Anglo-Indians attracted such obloquy, particularly from the memsahibs, may have been the sheer physical beauty of the women produced by such a mix. They were a constant reminder of sexual desire, a trait which late Victorian English men and women had come to deplore, both in themselves and in others.

The demise of the Company in India in 1858 was a watershed in many ways: whereas Company man was sensuous and emotional, as passionately devoted to his coterie of men friends as he would be to his bibi, his successor, Empire man, was essentially boyish, inspired by team games and team spirit, whilst at the same time hating physical contact and rampantly homophobic. Partly in response to the propaganda of the Company raj, which was inspired by the notion of a lofty distance between the ruler and the subject, partly because of the ever-present threat of mutiny, with its underlying threat of violation, but perhaps most of all because of the fervent religious morality being peddled by the missionaries, by the end of the nineteenth century the English had acquired an austere and self-denying character quite unrecogniseable from the sensuous and open-hearted people they had been two generations earlier.

Hook Swinging

Indian customs attracted the attention of the curious, and religious festivals and dramatic ceremonies exerted a fascination on the British throughout their time in India. John MacDonald describes 'hook swinging' graphically in 1770:

A rich man from Marr had prayed for children, and his wife had conceived a son: 'In return he publicly goes through a torment in honour of his Creator; and the pure and undefiled Gentoo religion; and his name is handed down to posterity amongst the worthy as a saint, and his family respected . . . An incision is made in each side, under his ribs,

to let in each hole a smooth iron hook, like those that let down a butt of beer to a cellar in London . . .With the irons in his side, he is drawn up in a moment with a pulley . . . So the music is playing, some are crying, others praying for him to get through his misery.

At the other end of the pole a rope is fixed, which a man takes hold of and runs him round three times.Whenever he was come to the same place they gave him a cheer . . . He was taken down in a moment, a cordial given, his wounds were dressed and he was carried home in triumph, with beatings of drums and music playing' (John MacDonald, Memoirs of an 18th Century Footman, Century, 1985). By the mid-nineteenth century, scenes such as that described were the subject of cheap paintings on mica, sold to passing travellers as postcards are today.

The problems of the Anglo-Indian continued well into the twentieth century, forming the basis of the fictional *Jewel in the Crown*, the film *Bhawani Junction*, and the real life of Merle Oberon, who felt compelled to keep her mixed British–Singhalese origins concealed for much of her Hollywood career. She eventually married an Argentinian and entertained the Duke of Edinburgh to dinner; that would never have happened in India.

COLONEL SKINNER

The hero of the Anglo-Indians was Colonel James Skinner, the son of a Scotsman and a Rajput princess. Barred by the decree of 1791 from joining the Company's service, he founded an irregular troop of cavalry known as Skinner's Horse, which conducted spectacular and adventurous operations in Northwest India, firstly as a mercenary outfit in the service of various potentates, then grudgingly readmitted to the Company's ranks. Although recognised for these exploits in the field, he was (and is still) revered for what he

Colonel Skinner's regimental 'durbar', a traditional Moghul practice he introduced to Skinner's Horse.

did to break down racial taboos. He was a man of great integrity and immense generosity, loved by all, and who behaved more like a gentleman than many of his English counterparts.

Skinner ran his cavalry in an unorthodox way, one innovation being the introduction of the durbar, or council, at which any of his soldiers could raise problems with senior officers. An adaptation of a Moghul tradition, the durbar gave Skinner an intimacy with his troops which in turn enhanced their own prestige. His friend William Fraser

(see page 92) became his second-in-command, and they frequently campaigned together.

Skinner fathered a substantial Anglo-Indian dynasty: according to his family he had seven wives, and according to legend, fourteen. He had eighty children – or, rather, eighty who claimed him as their father, one of whom, Elizabeth, turns up escaping from Delhi during the Mutiny. Husband and children in tow, she shoots her way through mutinous sepoys down the Grand Trunk Road, then, attacked by villagers, successfully invokes the name of her father to gain the assistance of the very sepoys she had just escaped. Concealed by a loyal soldier in a wagon, the party finally make it to the safety of Kurnaul where Elizabeth, neither fainting nor wilting like the rest of them, makes them all a nice pot of tea. Blood, albeit thinly spread, will out.

In appropriate multi-denominational style, Skinner built a mosque for one Muslim wife, a temple for another Hindu wife, then built his own church in Delhi, modestly dedicated to St James, where he was buried in 1841, near his friend Fraser.

SHARED CULTURES

The British gradually annexed not only Indian life itself, but representations of it. This great painting of the procession of Amar Singh of Tanjore featured the ruler of a once independent South Indian state; a year later, in 1798, he was pensioned off and exiled by the Company, who replaced him with his more pliant heir Sarabhoji (pictured in the smaller carriage). Sarabhoji himself was made a pensioned nobleman in 1799 and Tanjore became a regulation district in the Madras Presidency. The painting of Sarabhoji in procession in 1825 (opposite, below), shows the now purely nominal ruler of Tanjore shadowed by the ever-present British Resident resplendent on horseback (detail, opposite). But the British had long before worked their subtle magic on Sarabhoji, who had European tutors as a boy, spoke good English and had a European lifestyle, with a living room carpeted and furnished with English chairs, and opposite each other four bookcases filled chiefly with English books. Sarabhoji was also a keen patron of the arts, and commissioned numerous portraits of his family, in oils, in the Company style.

In general, the late eighteenth century saw a relaxed co-existence between the Company's servants and the native rulers. Many pleasures were shared, including displays by nautch dancers, music, poetry and cock fighting. Once the high moral tone demanded by the evangelists had taken hold, such idle distractions were frowned upon, and the easy intercourse between cultures disappeared. It is ironic to note that when the English were at their most corrupt and rapacious in relation to India they cut sympathetic figures in general, and enjoyed a certain level of integration with native society at all levels. However, as they became less corrupt, but more moralistic, religious and wedded to high ideals of service and improvement in India, they became worthier but less appealing characters, increasingly distanced from the Indians themselves.

The procession of Amar Singh of Tanjore, c. 1797, with Sarabhoji ominously leading the way.

A dour Company resident keeps a watchful eye on the puppet ruler Sarabhoji, c. 1825.

Sarabhoji on parade in 1825. He replaced Amar Singh as ruler of Tanjore at the instigation of the Company.

Other Europeans arrived in India, often military men in the service of notional or actual enemies of the Company, particularly in the troublesome Mahratta Confederation in the west. Some opted for a more civilised, leisurely life: in the late eighteenth century, Lucknow, capital of the Kingdom of Oudh, was considered a city of high culture and sophisticated pleasures, and attracted not only the Company's servants for trade, but European adventurers.

One such, the French Colonel Polier, had helped design the fortifications of Fort William, Calcutta, before falling foul of the Company's new strictures concerning foreign nationals. He retreated to Lucknow where he studied oriental culture and took three concubines. His friend Colonel Martin, a Swiss, had joined the Company's army after the defeat of the French at Pondicherry in 1761, and eventually rose to the rank of major general whilst at the same time superintending the King of Oudh's armoury. Colonel Polier built luxurious palaces, kept four concubines, collected oriental manuscripts and patronised painters.

ARCHITECTURE

The Company entered the East not as colonists but merchants, and their early buildings reflected that utilitarian function. In the Far East, the lightly defended factory and its appendages remained the standard until the end of the eighteenth century, whilst in India the need to fortify the factory created a new style of Company building. Fort St George in Madras was the first; work commenced in 1639, and by the nineteenth century it had all the requirements of a small garrison town within its walls: church, bank, auction room, theatre and arsenal.

After the destruction of the Calcutta settlement by Siraj-ud-dualah, the Company vowed never to be caught out in like manner again. Fort William was built as a stronghold capable in times of crisis of accommodating the entire European community of the city. Self-sufficient in matters both spiritual (the garrison church of St Peter lies within its walls) and temporal (wells, granaries and a gunpowder store were all to be found there), the fort was a model of state-of-the-art European fortification theory, with ramparts, redoubts and a huge expanse of jungle uprooted to allow a clear line of fire.

During the Company's time, buildings were designed by artillery officers, residents, mathematicians and clergymen – in short, anyone but architects, who remained resolutely at home. As a result, many of the buildings had an endearingly amateur air, the product of enthusiasm and necessity rather than expertise and commission. Surprisingly little attempt was made to integrate Indian architectural ideas, which were considered decidedly un-Christian. The only Company building to reflect anything of its locality was the famous granary, the Gola at Patna, a grand statement of benign intent, built to keep famine forever from the province of Bihar. It was modelled on similar, but much smaller granaries in the region. It never functioned properly, but drew interested visitors, including a Nepalese prince who rode up its hundred-foot staircase and down the other side.

Government House at Lahore did reflect Moghul architecture – in this case by appropriating it wholesale. The tomb of a cousin of Akbar the Great was adapted as part of the residency, the domed mausoleum making an ideal dining room, and the sarcophagus a perfect kitchen table.

The development of the architecture of the Presidencies matched the scale of the Company's achievements – and ambitions – in India. The chosen style for post-Plassey building was neo-classical, long after the Gothic revival had started back home. The clear lines, imposing pediments and dazzling whiteness of the buildings in Calcutta and Madras were designed to convey all the dignity and power of their Greek and Roman antecedents. Even the homes of the merchants were imbued with the same sensibility, anticipating a triumphant return to England, to wealth, respectability and a stately pile. By the very end of the Company's raj some Gothic influence had crept into buildings such as Calcutta Cathedral, completed in 1847, but by this time the British had been seized with an evangelical Christian vigour which rendered the pagan allusions of classicism quite redundant.

The Mutiny and subsequent absorption of the Company by the Crown ensured that the Company's servants never had to put up with the oppressive fussiness of Indo-Victorian-Gothic, more suited to a blasted heath than a July monsoon: that dubious honour fell to the Pukka imperialists. In its wilder Indo-Saracenic mode, later English architecture in India fell victim to an incoherent eclecticism: Lutyens, one of the few professional architects to be commissioned to build there, called it the 'mad riot of the tom tom', which says much for his taste but little for his knowledge of Indian classical percussion.

CRAFTSMEN

Local Indian craftsmen quickly responded to the requirements of the English merchants living in India, and to those of their distant customers. Furniture was especially in demand, since the Indian way of sitting, eating and sleeping was alien to Europeans, and in due course 'progressive' Indian rulers began to emulate Company grandees, which created further demand. Some items of furniture evolved specifically for the comfort of the Company's servants in the East – planter's chairs, fans, wicker chairs and sofas, and cane blinds.

Many pieces were also designed to be easily portable, as long, arduous journeys were almost unavoidable for those in military or civil service under the Company. Portable beds known as cots, writing desks, and the range of 'campaign furniture' evolved, often designed to protect valuables such as dinner services, medicines and wine bottles. The drinks cabinet was held in particularly high esteem by the hard-drinking officers of the Company's armies.

The southern coastal town of Vizagapatam specialised in manufacturing furniture with ivory carving and elaborate carved patterns filled with black lacquer for decoration. The technique was used for writing boxes, desks and other large items of furniture, as well as for the ubiquitous tea caddy.

The lavish lifestyles of the English in India created niche markets which only Europeans could fill: silversmiths sprang up in the Presidencies,

European-owned and managed, but with specially trained Indian craftsmen working for them. The products were virtually indistinguishable from their European equivalents.

Metal bidri ware from the Deccan, though not a significant export item, was appreciated by the Company employees who had taken up smoking the hookah. A sophisticated technique involving zinc alloys, it enabled extremely fine decorative motifs to be created in metal.

A bidri ware hookah bowl, showing the intricate decorative possibilities of the technique.

THE PAISLEY SHAWL

The origins of the design known today as Paisley, and the spread of its popularity through the Kashmir shawl, is an extraordinary example of a global cross-pollination of ideas, in which the Company played a significant role.

The design originally represented the Chaldean date palm, which also symbolised the Tree of Life. It was adopted across Indo-European civilisations, and although it became extinct under the Greeks and Romans, the design remained a popular theme in Indian art, where it was first adapted for use on shawls in about 1600. The oldest surviving fragment shows the slight tilt at the top of the motif which led to its fanciful name, 'the teardrop of Allah', or, more prosaically, the 'tadpole'. Kashmir shawls were one of the prized possessions of the rulers of India – who were not known for their austerity – and were made from a cloth woven from the fine downy pashmina (or undercoat) of a certain Himalayan goat, *Capra Hircus*, known as the shawl goat. When spring arrives, the goat rubs its pashmina off on rocks or trees, and the hair, collected in the wild, is woven into a cloth which, though very light, is also very warm. The weavers, especially those of Kashmir, created what were known as 'ring' shawls because they were so fine they could pass through a ring. Decorated using an elaborate twill-tapestry technique, they could take as much as a year and a half to make.

The Company had been made aware of the value of shawls early on. The ever-correct Sir Thomas Roe (see page 18) had been offered 'a Gold Shalh' as a gift by the Moghul Governor at Surat but had spurned it as a bribe: 'I answered we were but newly friends: when I saw any constancy in his carriage . . . I would be more free with him, yet I would receive no obligation.' In the 1700s, an officer of the East India Company obtained a shawl as a gift for his wife at home, and other officers followed suit. It soon became apparent to the Company that here was a commercial opportunity, but the problem was one of supply; the fine wild pashmina was scarce, and goats raised in captivity produced coarser hair. Most Kashmiri weavers produced shawls made of the coarser hair, but if customers in England wanted wild pashmina instead, they could end up paying some £300, the equivalent then of the price of a house in Berkeley Square.

As the trade developed, attempts were made – unsuccessfully – to import shawl goats to England. European woollen manufacturers also tried to create adequate imitations. The French were the first, using designs copied from *Le Cashmerien*, a publication showing the designs of genuine Kashmir shawls owned by the French aristocracy.

A fragment of what may be the earliest shawl to be brought back to England c. 1680 by a Company servant.

Capra Hircus, the shawl goat. Native of the Himalayas, its downy winter undercoat gave the prized pashmina wool.

Edinburgh and Norwich were for a short while rival centres for the nascent shawl industry in Britain, 'in imitation of the Indian', but after 1808 manufacturing focused on the Scottish town of Paisley, just south of Glasgow. The 'ten-box lay' was invented there, which allowed multicoloured weaves to be easily produced, and factories were able to produce imitations of the Kashmir designs within days of fresh examples arriving from India. Priced at around £12, the Paisley shawls swiftly became hugely popular, and even reached Turkey and the Middle East.

In 1821, William Moorcroft (see page 10), who had earlier attempted to bring a herd of shawl goats and their 'golden fleece' back to England, had shown a few Paisley samples to Kashmiri weavers. They were impressed by the precision with which the designs had been followed, but less convinced by the quality of the cloth and weave. Once again, the Company set out to track down supplies of pashmina, but failed to make progress, and attempts to obtain goats floundered likewise. Meanwhile, Moorcroft was making detailed copies of the designs used by Kashmiri weavers, which he brought back to England. These show a distinct evolution from the simple beginnings, with a more pronounced teardrop shape and far more elaborate loops and whorls.

The Paisley shawl became one of the great fashion success stories of the nineteenth century, and although the designs on the shawls themselves were frequently pirated from India or other European manufacturers, the price and quality of the Scottish product ensured their pre-eminence. The Chaldean Tree of Life had been metamorphosed into Paisley, a design as at home in the gentlemen's clubs of St James as it was to become in the age of psychedelia.

PAINTERS OF THE INDIAN SCENE

The detractors and the defenders of the East India Company in India tend to conduct their battles on the field of political and military affairs. As a result, one area in which the English made a significant contribution is generally passed over except by those with a particular interest in the arts. Ironically, the expertise of the Moghuls in painting, literature, music and architecture is often treated as some cultural high watermark, as though vindicating their imperial rule, whilst the more modest contribution of the English to the cultural scene is generally ignored. Nonetheless, there is no doubt about the thoroughness and zeal with which they went about cataloguing their new-found Empire. They were perhaps moved by that same desire to express possession through art that motivated that earlier development of English painting, the depiction of the landowner in his country estate and portraits of great houses, which was without obvious parallel in continental Europe. The English psyche was acquisitive in its aesthetics as well as in respect of territory, which may in part account for their unparalleled success in the latter.

The Moghul Court, especially under Akbar, Jehangir and Shah Jehan, had an extremely active tradition of painting, producing miniatures and other works of astonishing virtuosity. Much of this rich heritage was still in evidence at the time when the Company started to make its influence felt on the subcontinent.

Moti Singh, Maharawal of Udaipur. The photograph was hand coloured after printing.

Indian figures on the banks of the Ganges, painted by William Prinsep.

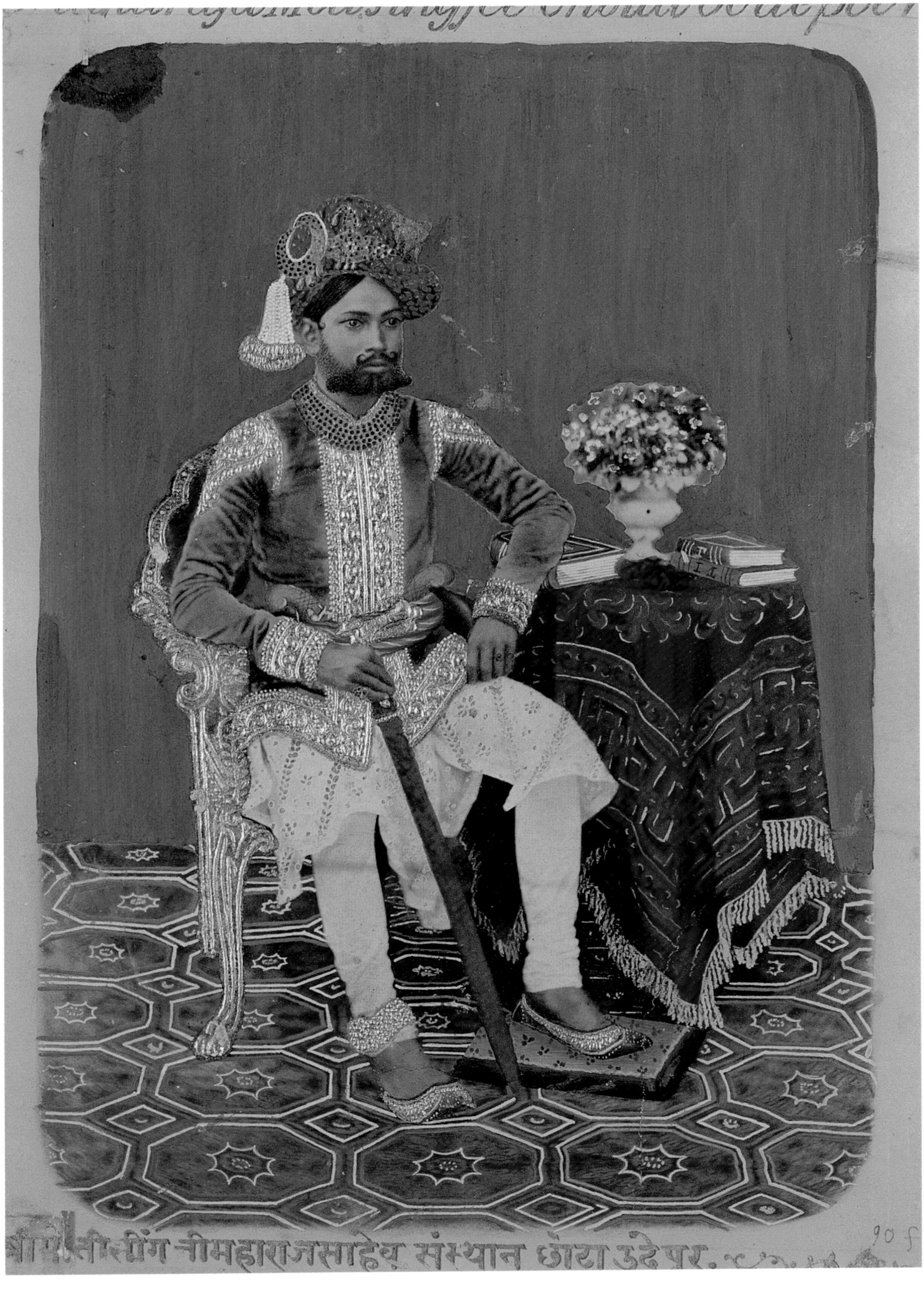
महाराजसाहेब संस्थान छोटा उदेपर.

A portrait of an Indian gentleman dressed in the western style. Late 1840s.

A London-made silver centrepiece presented to Captain Charles McLeod of Hyderabad upon his retirement in 1853.

The English, inheriting the talented pool of painters previously in the service of Moghul patrons, put it to work to depict those aspects of Indian life which fascinated them. Natural history and architecture were initially the favourite subjects, and a particularly happy marriage of Moghul artistic sensibility and western patronage emerged, known as the Company School. For an artistic tradition long accustomed to the meticulous detail required for the rendition of a bird or insect in miniature form for Moghul patrons, the demands of enthusiastic Englishmen were relatively easy to meet, and the natural history paintings of the Company School combine the observational powers and technical brilliance of the Moghul School with the dry, clincial eye of a western observer. Sir Elijah and Lady Impey (see page 154) were avid patrons of the School, and had three Patna artists in their employ, including Shaikh Zayn-al-Dyn, who painted the Mango bird (the Indian blackheaded oriole) illustrated opposite.

Where architecture was concerned, Indian painters were frequently asked to render in two dimensions what their forebears had built in three, and wonderfully detailed paintings of the decorations of the temples and monuments of the subcontinent were the result. The English passion for ethnography and the accurate depiction of the differences between tribes, castes and occupations was, however, not something that the Moghuls had been particularly interested in; local artists were able to turn their hand to such subjects with fine, if variable, results. Less successful were their attempts to convey the Indian landscape in the tradition of European classical landscape painters; perspective proved elusive, and their attempts, though charming, can look rather comical to the western eye.

The first European painters to come to India filled this void: the depiction of landscape, and of architecture accurately but atmospherically conveyed within that landscape, became the principal and most fertile field of activity for artists such as William Hodges, William Prinsep, Thomas and William Daniell, and numerous others. The accuracy of their renditions of Indian scenes was, however, often undermined by the influence of the picturesque tradition, which allowed for the rearrangement of the subject if it did not conform to certain ideals. Ironically, the same aesthetic sense acted to mute the sheer exuberance and exoticism of the scene, so that the results sometimes appear flatter and duller – in short, more western – than might be expected. George Chinnery was one artist who remained slightly

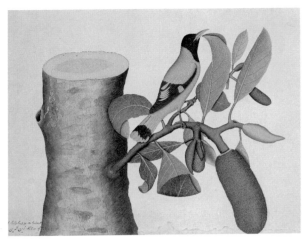

A mango bird on a jack fruit. A painting once in the collection of the Impeys, pioneer patrons of the Company School.

Grasshoppers depicted in the style of the Company School by Seeta Ram.

Captain Linneas Tripe's View of the Nave from Simhasanum, Madura.

outside this commercial tradition, mainly supporting himself through portraiture; his landscapes are more intimate and more subtle than those of his peers, who were drawn to the better-known and more spectacular scenes. Whatever the merits of the result, the century leading up to the Company's dissolution saw the largest effort ever undertaken by one culture to depict another.

Back home, it was inevitable that the Company's successes after Plassey should attract the attention of the emerging Historical School of painting. In the early 1760s, visitors to Vauxhall Gardens, the fashionable London pleasure gardens, were 'entertained' by large canvasses by Francis Hayman depicting victories by Wolfe in Canada, the British navy triumphant against the French, Clive at Plassey, Eyre Coote and numerous other victorious generals. 'History painting' was full of grandeur, classical allusion, and, supposedly, great attention to contemporary

detail. Benjamin West, Robert Home and William Devis were among the exponents of the School, and they found in India suitable themes for their work. The death of Tipu Sultan at Seringapatam (see page 138) provided the last of the great subjects for this School, until 'history painting' was suddenly and dramatically revived by the Mutiny.

J M W Turner made some watercolours from George White's drawings, *Views in India*. The results, whilst unmistakably Turner, are less obviously India, and Turner remained ignorant of the East. Richard Westall, a fellow painter who had travelled in India, once humbly pointed out to Turner that the palm trees in a tropical painting of his could not have turned an autumnal yellow but should be repainted green. The master responded, 'Umph! I can't afford it! I can't afford it!' and left the palm fronds yellow.

J M W Turner's The Snowy Range, *based on a drawing by Lt G F White.*

The Daniells

Thomas and William Daniell were an uncle and nephew team who, influenced by the earlier work of William Hodges, saw a potential niche for artists of their technical ability to depict the landscapes of the previously almost unknown India. They sailed in an East India Company vessel which, with a longwindedness characteristic of sea voyages of the time, went first to Canton before finally depositing them in Calcutta in 1786. The Daniells stayed in India until 1793, recording Calcutta in detail and making three hazardous trips to areas as yet unexplored by Europeans. They refined their technique so that they were able quickly to record images through sketches, work them up into full paintings, and then engrave them back in London. Their most famous work, Oriental Scenery, includes 144 plates. In this painting we see William gazing at the fort at Bijaigargh through a telescope while his uncle sketches and their servants erect an awning. By their later standards, this was a minimal crew: the entourage on their southern tour of 1792 totalled forty-four.

PHOTOGRAPHY

The appearance of photography in India gave a new impetus to the recording of the Indian scene, and was swiftly adopted on the subcontinent: the Photographic Society of Bombay was founded in 1854, only a year later than its London counterpart. The earliest known photographs taken in India come from an amateur album dating from about 1843, which, although of no great technical merit, are fascinating for the way they evoke this era, distant in time, culture and geography, in a modern medium. Photography quickly replaced painting as a way of recording architectural and ethnographical subjects, and army officers and surgeons in the Company's service were often well placed to cover a great diversity of subjects. From 1855, students at the Company's military academy at Addiscombe in England were taught the principles of photography.

From an album containing the oldest known photographs of India, taken by an English lady based in Uttar Pradesh.

Captain Linnaeus Tripe was an officer in the Company's Madras army, and his fine images of the temples of Madura show contrasting light and shade as well as great detail, whilst Dr John Murray's waxed paper negative of the Taj Mahal (opposite) casts a different light on a subject made familiar by painters from earlier times.

Portrait photography became popular with the Indian aristocracy and middle classes, while the socially concerned were able to record the ghastly effects of plague and starvation on the previously faceless millions. Photographs also recorded the destruction caused by the Mutiny of 1857, and gave credibility to subjects which might otherwise have seemed fanciful, such as this picture of the fish-shaped 'Royal Boat of Oude' moored on the Gumpti at Lucknow.

The fantastical fish-shaped Royal Boat of Oude at Lucknow in 1857, with the pulverised British Residency in the background.

Print from a wax paper negative of the Taj Mahal, dating from 1854.

LIFE UNDER THE COMPANY RAJ

> *'A lively life, with the thermometer at several hundred!'*
>
> Emily Eden

THE DEMON DRINK

The factors of the Company had a capacity for hard liquor which would hospitalise the modern *bon viveur*. Even the diarist William Hickey, no slouch when it came to drink, was amazed by a dinner he attended in an officers' mess in Calcutta, calling it '. . . the most sustained debauch I had seen in my life'. A third of all illness among Company employees was liver-related. There were many reasons for these excesses — one was that good-quality drinking water was hard to find, and alcohol was widely believed to kill germs — but the most common must have been sheer boredom. A young man, stuck in an isolated factory with the same companions for years on end, or in the mofussil (country) with two or three couples for company, was ever prey to tedium: 'How some of these young men must detest their lives! Mr —— was brought up entirely at Naples and Paris, came out in the world when he was quite a boy, and cares for nothing but society and Victor Hugo's novels . . . '(Emily Eden, *Letters from India*, ed. Eleanor Eden, London, 1872).

Arrack (grain, rice or other spirits) and toddy (fermented palm sap) were cheap and powerful, but that did not rule out further refinements of the route to insensibility. The infamous Hog Lane in Canton was the spiritual home of a particularly vicious cocktail made from alcohol, tobacco juice, sugar and arsenic. More aristocratic was punch — containing arrack mixed with sugar, citrus juice, water and spices — its five ingredients giving the name of the drink its Sanskrit root, in the same way that its five rivers gave the Punjab its name.

'Sale of English Beauties in the East Indies', a typically cruel caricature of the 'Fishing Fleet' by Rowlandson.

CHAPTER XI

Soldiers, predictably, had a reputation for being the heaviest drinkers. John Macdonald noted that 'When an English soldier goes on guard, he takes two bottles of arrack to drink in the night' (*Memoirs of an 18th Century Footman*, Century 1985). But their officers and the other Company servants were not far behind: at one dinner party fourteen people managed to consume forty-two bottles of claret and the same of Madeira.

Claret, Madeira, champagne and port were shipped out in large quantities from the earliest days, but as the Company became more established in India and the Far East, home products were also exported. Beer was popular, and useful as a safe source of liquid for crew and passengers on the long voyage east, as it was difficult to store water for long periods. However, the dark porter which was commonly drunk in the seventeenth and early eighteenth century did not travel well, especially through the tropics, and was not particularly refreshing in the baking heat.

It was impossible to brew beer in hot climates until the introduction of refrigeration in the mid-nineteenth century, as wild yeast strains would taint the warm brew. Brewers at home started to experiment with a lighter, more heavily hopped beer designed to travel well. The most successful of these was India Ale, a pale, sparkling bitter which was first brewed in 1752 by the London brewer George Hodgson, who was based in Bow on the River Lea, close to the Company's dockyards. By 1800, the brewery was sending nearly a thousand barrels a year to the East, and by 1813, four times that amount, taking advantage of the low shipping rates for outgoing vessels – the freight charge for sending a barrel to Calcutta was the same as sending one to Edinburgh. Charrington's evolved an equivalent product they called Pale Ale.

The big Burton breweries became keen to emulate their success, and when two employees of the East India Company suggested that Alsopp's (one of the Burton group) try to reproduce the Hodgson's ale, their head brewer, Job Goodhead, brewed what became famous as East India Pale Ale (later shortened to India Pale Ale or IPA). Others quickly followed suit, and William Bateman, whose family had long been associated with the Company, secured the contract to supply the Indian army; by the 1830s the sales of Bass ales were up 50 per cent, largely attributable to the 5,000 barrels of IPA being shipped annually to Calcutta alone. By 1850, 65 per cent of their total production of 78,000 barrels was in the form of IPA.

The Pickled Factory

The factors and other servants at Bencoolen in Sumatra prompted a mild rebuke from the Directors (the Company settled all the mess bills of its factories) when they consumed the following in July 1716:

74 dozen bottles of wine
24 dozen bottles of beer
42 gallons of Madeira
6 flasks of Shiraz
274 bottles of toddy
3 leaguers and 3 quarters of arrack
164 gallons of Goa toddy

The association of gin with tonic was due essentially to the East India Company. The use of distilled spirit flavoured with juniper (the English word 'gin' is a contraction of the French *genièvre*), was first recorded in England for medicinal purposes. Samuel Pepys took a strong draught of gin to cure a stomach disorder in 1663. By the turn of the century, however, crude gin – often added to cordials – was starting to rival beer as the everyday alcohol of the masses, its strength and relatively low price contributing to its abuse, which was of rising social concern in the first half of the eighteenth century.

In the meantime, the first exports of gin were being sent to the East as ballast in the Company's outgoing EastIndiamen. Some casks were mistakenly returned, and were prized for the flavour imparted by their long maturation, the gentle action of the waves, and the changes wrought by the climate; this rare, modified gin was know as East India gin.

Gin's pretensions as a medicinal drink lost credibility through the damage it had wrought on the health of the lower orders in the 1740s and 1750s, but by the 1760s, the shadows of 'Gin Lane' and 'Mother's Ruin' had been dispelled, and unrefined gin had given way to refined 'dry' gin, which was gradually to gain in popularity over the next century. However, it was Indian tonic water that really brought gin back into fashion. The medicinal value of the bark of the South American cinchona tree was known to earlier physicians, but the specific anti-malarial properties of the extract of quinine were first noted in the 1820s. In that lay a preventive to the scourge of malaria which so debilitated the colonies in the East. Plantations of cinchona were successfully established by the Company in Ceylon and later India, and Indian tonic water was devised to provide a regular preventative dose. Unfortunately, the astringent taste of quinine rendered it unpalatable on its own, and the problem was solved by the simple expedient of adding a measure of gin. This perfect mix, being visually indistinguishable from pure tonic water, also made it ideal for those who felt like a sun-downer at midday. Gin and tonic became the archetypal drink of the British Empire, and its popularity remains undimmed today – an estimated sixty-five per cent of all gin drunk worldwide is mixed with tonic.

The Company's servants made other, more imaginative uses of gin. Singapore, newly founded by Stamford Raffles, had its own Raffles Sling; a Gimlet (gin, lime juice and sugar) was a favourite in the Himalayas; and there were Penang and Javan variants of the Singapore Sling. This long-standing association of gin, and particularly of London Dry Gin, with the heyday of colonialism accounts for the domi-nance of British gin brands in the world today.

HOOKAH AND CHEROOTS

The cultivation of tobacco had been introduced into India by Akbar the Great during the sixteenth century, and by the time the Company arrived was already well established. Indian men, and sometimes women too, smoked hookahs, in which tobacco was flavoured with molasses and kept alight with a glowing charcoal, the smoke passing through a water bowl to cool and filter it. The hookah prompted many panegyrics from contemporary writers of the time: 'It is a friend in whose Bosom we may repose our most confiden-tial secrets; and a Counsellor upon whose advice we may rely in our most important Concerns . . . the Music of its sound puts the warblings of the Nightingale to Shame, and the Fragrance of its perfume brings a Blush on the Cheek of a Rose' (Anon, seventeenth century). Smoking a hookah was widely adopted by the Company's servants early on, although its use died out with the arrival of the more con-servative memsahib, and was replaced by the cheroot, a cigar with two closed ends which was also commonly smoked by both Indian men and women. Cheroots came from South India, or, better still, from Manila.

A Company painting of a bibi sitting on a western chair, contentedly smoking a hookah.

THE HEAT

'We have had very hot winds and delightfully cool houses. Everyone uses tatties now . . . Tatties are however dangerous when you are obliged to go abroad, the heat acts so powerfully on the body that you are commonly affected with a severe catarrh' (Letter from Dr Cambell, Calcutta, 1789, in Carey, *Good Old Days*). The effects of modern air-conditioning are much the same. Tatties were dampened screens hung over all the openings of a house. Made of cuscus, a grass from the dry areas of India, the technology was apparently invented by Akbar the Great, and given the climate of India, this invention alone may have accounted for his greatness in the eyes of his subjects.

The Moghuls themselves constructed tykhana, cool rooms dug under their palaces which provided some refuge from the fierce summer heat. William Fraser (see page 90), Assistant Resident in Delhi after 1806, demolished the

A group of men on an Indian verandah. The monkey is kindly offering the lounging man a cheroot.

palace of a nobleman to create his own residence, but kept the tykhana, with the result that his guests rarely complained of the heat in their correspondence.

If keeping the heat out was difficult, then cold could always be brought in: an American entrepreneur, Frederick Tudor, shipped 180 tonnes of New England ice to Calcutta in 1833, wasting 60 tonnes during the 4-month voyage and another 20 up the Hooghli. Despite the loss, it was an improvement on the hill ice – brought down at great inconvenience – that the British in India were used to: native ice was 6d a pound, and Tudor was able to sell at half that.

Although the loyalty of the English to their woollen uniforms was cursed by every common soldier in the East, they did manage to invent the pith helmet, which was to become a symbol of English colonialism. It was a practical piece of headgear designed in the early nineteenth century to minimise the effect of the scorching sun, and replaced the felt hats of earlier times. The helmet later acquired subtle variations in shape according to region.

DEATH, DISEASE AND REMEDIES

Dr John Lind's *Essay on Diseases*, published in 1768, reckoned Bengal was one of the unhealthiest places on earth, and advised men to 'chew rhubarb, stop his nose with linen dipped in camphor and vinegar, and drink a concoction of bark [probably cinchona], garlic, and rhubarb in brandy'. The brandy was a nice touch: alcohol was the single most significant contributory factor to the death rate in India as a whole, combined with lack of exercise and an unbalanced diet.

The rate of attrition was ferociously high throughout the Company's time. The variety of means by which a man could be carried off was quite bewildering. Malaria, typhoid or enteric fever, cholera, dysentry and smallpox were the most common diseases, and the bites of scorpions and mad dogs were frequently lethal. Snakes were an ever-present threat in the home – as much in the cities as in the mofussil. Barriers of tin, broken glass, wire mesh and carbolic powder were the standard defences, but snakes sometimes fell out of the rafters, onto the heads of those below, or were trampled underfoot. The frequency of death bred a certain indifference to grief; one doctor remarked to the mother of a child just lost to lockjaw, 'Thank God I have no wife or children to bother me. Good night' (H Tytler, *An Englishwoman in India*, ed. A Sattin, Oxford and New York, 1986).

The Company's trading activities took its servants to countries and climates vastly different from their own, and exposed them to health risks which their own herbal and medical traditions were quite unable to deal with. However, just as they adopted or adapted the language, customs and culture of the countries to which they were posted, the more enlightened servants of the Company learned much from native herbal traditions, particularly those of India and China. Up until the eighteenth century, when chemical and biochemical treatments started to form the basis of modern medicine, the West, too, had depended on herbal remedies – plants were the only source of drugs, whether for the treatment of specific medical conditions or for use as a general tonic. When the traders of the East India Company started to bring exotic herbs and spices back to Europe, western botanists and herbalists alike were fascinated, and many made the voyage out to the East in order to identify and classify these new plants. Eventually the role of the apothecary – essentially someone who dealt in herbs and plants – was superseded by that of the pharmacist, who isolated and utilised active substances in treatments – but until that time the Company performed a valuable service in bringing new herbs, spices and plants into use.

Many plants used in modern herb-based health products owe their introduction to the West to the activities of the Company. The case of aloe vera is typical: now a staple of the skin-care industry, and cultivated worldwide, aloes were highly prized in ancient Greece as a purgative. The island of Socotra, off the Horn of Africa, was the only known source of aloes in the ancient world, and Aristotle is reputed to have suggested to Alexander the Great that he

An intricate 19th-century boxwood model of a Chinese apothecary's shop.

conquer the island for its aloes alone. When Captain Keeling visited Socotra in 1608, he bought a tonne of aloes for export to the constipated East, and subsequently aloes were imported into England as well; they were on sale through London druggists in 1693. Interest from botanists stimulated wider cultivation, initially in the Cape, but later in Curaçao and the West Indies.

From the contacts with the Chinese at Canton, the Company learnt about those most prized health products, royal jelly and ginseng. Although now widely cultivated, ginseng was originally a rare wild plant from Manchuria and Korea, valued as a panacea. The trade in roots was strictly controlled, and even became the cause of wars. It would appear that westerners had become familiar with this efficacious plant at an early stage in the development of East-West trade, since American ginseng was being exported to China as early as 1718 by Canadian Jesuits. The nineteenth-century boxwood model illustrated here, made for the export market, shows in great detail a traditional Chinese medicine shop. At the back of the shop is an inscription which would not be out of place in its modern equivalent: 'In this shop all types of dietary remedies, acupuncture and moxicombustion.' That most successful of the Company's trading commodities, tea, had long been used in China as a herbal infusion, and much of its early popularity in England was based on the health claims made for it, frequently exaggerated. Today, green tea has been re-adopted by the health industry, following the positive results of recent research into its anti-oxidant qualities.

THE HILL STATION

The hill station, that airy refuge from the blistering summer heat of the plains, remains one of the archetypal images of British India, but it reached it apotheosis during the Empire, after the Company's time. A few hardy souls during the early nineteenth century built houses in the hills, but they were seen as pioneering eccentrics. In 1822, Captain Charles Kennedy built himself a glorified log cabin in Simla, in which he entertained in some style those intrepid enough to visit him. The small town in the hills north of Delhi may

have seemed like the back of beyond then, but Kennedy obviously had an eye for location, for by 1827 the Earl of Amherst, perhaps still smarting from his ill-fated mission to Peking (see page 40), inaugurated it as a 'vice-regal sanitorium'. Within fifty years Simla had become the imperial capital during the summer months, as the Viceroy and other civil servants, the military, and 'grass widows' (ladies whose unfortunate husbands continued to toil in the heat and dust below) decamped there from the plains. Christchurch was completed in 1857, and the Mall (below) became the fashionable place to parade of an evening. Ootacamund in the Kunda Hills was pioneered by John Sullivan, Collector of Coimbatore, who spent most of his time in his fine stone house there, neglecting his official posting and prompting a stern reprimand from his superiors.

The fashionable Mall in Simla, 1860, shortly after the Company's demise.

TRAVEL BY RIVER

The rivers of the East provided natural arteries by which the rigours of land travel could be avoided. As the Company expanded out of Bengal towards Delhi, the Ganges lent itself particularly well to stately river journeys, and the Brahmaputra later gave ready access to the tea plantations of Assam. In the early nineteenth century, boats were usually hired privately; the larger ones, as much as twenty metres long, were equipped with masts and sails and, for emergencies, oarsmen. Airy cabins sat on the top deck from which to view the endless spectacles offered by river life – ruined temples, crocodiles, cremations, etc – with servant quarters below. The smaller 'budgerows' had to tow a boat behind with the supplies. The development of steamships gave rise to regular scheduled shipping lines which could be quite luxurious – meals were served in a saloon in which 'the tables were covered with starched white cloths, the china and silver marked with the Company's crest . . . ' (J and R Godden, *Two Under the Indian Sun*, New York, 1966).

THE FISHING FLEET

In the early days of the Company women rarely made the voyage out to the East; berths were scarce, the journey arduous and unpredictable, and there was no prospect of a suitable life when they arrived. Probably the first Englishwoman to do so was Mrs Hudson and her maid Frances in 1617, as companions to an Armenian lady of Indian birth. As the Company gained a foothold, however, the Directors recognised that its less senior servants, and particularly the soldiers, could not be eternally parted from the company of 'civilised' women; they were also concerned at the ease with which their servants took up with Indian bibi, or, worst of all, married the Catholic daughters of Portuguese. In the 1670s, they inaugurated a trial assisted-passage scheme to Madras, but it was not a roaring success; although they helped initially with accommodation, unless a woman secured a husband pretty smartly she was left to her own devices, which usually meant marriage to an Indian or Eurasian, prostitution ('gone sour'), or ignominiously being 'returned empty' to England. Part of the problem was that the 'Fishing Fleet', as it was known,

tended to consist of, at a generous estimation, those of 'limited charms and beauty', or, less generously, of women 'of shrivelled and dry description . . . educated merely to cover the surface of their mental deformity'. In any case, there was precious little to offer them, particularly in India: for wives of low-ranking soldiers, the life of squalor and hardship that greeted them was scarcely different from the one they had left.

The Directors swiftly dropped the scheme, preferring instead to lambast the lax morals of the women whom they had themselves brought to that condition. 'Whereas some of these women are grown scandalous to our nation, religion and Government interest, we require you to give them fair warning that they apply themselves to a more sober and Christian conversation' (Court of Directors to the Deputy Governor of Bombay, 1675). But the precedent was set, and over the next century the 'Fishing Fleet' achieved something like respectability: after all, fortunes were being made in the Company's service, which created waves of eligibility; somebody would usually be more than willing to invite their cousin, nièce or sister to visit them; and Calcutta was not necessarily the graveyard of matrimonial ambition. A Madame le Grand appeared there in the 1780s, to much acclaim and scandal, and later re-emerged on the historical stage as Princess Talleyrand, wife of Napoleon's estranged Foreign Minister and châtelaine of Haut-Brion, one of the finest Bordeaux vineyards. The fate of Monsieur le Grand is not recorded. As the fleet arrived at one or other Presidency, unmarried young men would descend from the mofussil; balls would be arranged, visiting cards left, and courtships swiftly conducted, for the men wanted wives and the women had not journeyed all the way to India for their own amusement. There was another reason for speed: a white complexion was considered highly desirable, and it was reckoned that women had forty days to capture the attention of a match before they lost their pallour.

The 'Fishing Fleet' had its drawbacks, but at least had the advantage of what-you-see-is-what-you-get. A long engagement with a girl from back home, whilst waiting for the requisite promotion, could be risky. One such lady finally arrived to marry her husband: 'Good heavens!' he cried, seeing how she corpulent she had become '. . . am I expected to marry all that?' (F Marryatt, *Gup*, London 1868).

COMPANY AT WAR

> '*I saw myself founding a new religion, marching into Asia riding an elephant, a turban on my head, and in my hands a new Koran I would have written to suit my needs.*'
>
> Napoleon Bonaparte

THE INDIAN ARMY

London always lay at the centre of the East India Company's operations – at least in theory. Given the operational and logistical problems of trying to run an enterprise half a globe away, it was more often the exigencies of the field that determined the way the Company was actually run. Nowhere was this more true than in the military in India, where the situation was further complicated by the involvement of Crown troops in the Company's wars.

The Company's raj in India has been called a 'garrison state' in which the military underwrote commercial and territorial ambitions. With at most 125,000 European men, women and children among a native population of 250 million, the garrisons must at times have seemed in a state of perpetual siege; but through a combination of skill, luck and unwavering self-belief, the conquerors managed to convince the conquered of their invincibility.

The military organisation of the Company in India appears at first sight bafflingly complex. At any one time the Company might deploy native troops (sepoys) of its Indian army; European troops of the same army; troops of the British army stationed in India and subsidised by the Company; forces of Indian princes or states in alliance with the Company; and irregular cavalry or troops formally or informally associated with the Company. This complexity is a reflection of the ad hoc evolution of the forces. Initially, there was little requirement for any significant defensive force; the Bombay Presidency then inherited the rump of a disbanded Crown regiment left over from an undeclared war against the Moghuls; following this, Crown troops joined with the Company's own and new sepoy regiments, as well as those of local rulers in alliance, to ward off the threat of French activities in the Carnatic; and after Plassey (in 1557), these threads were all woven together to form the Bengal army, which achieved its first decisive victory at Buxar in 1764.

In the mid-eighteenth century, southern India suffered an extension of the struggles between France and England in Europe and North America, and the formative years of the Indian army were largely driven by the need to respond to the political and strategic pressures of the war with France between 1740 and 1748, and the machinations of the French Governor of Pondicherry, Joseph Dupleix, whose cunning alliances with regional rulers threatened the Company's existence in the Carnatic. The relationship between the Company and the Crown was thus mutually, if grudgingly, interdependent: the Company needed additional military support, and the Crown could not afford to let France achieve supremacy in India, or, for that matter, further east. The French had pioneered the use of the sepoy – a word ultimately derived from the Urdu 'sipahi' – an Indian soldier in the service of the French or British. In time and with training, the sepoys became the mainstay of the Company's armies. The capture of Manila in the Philippines in 1762, in the Company's name and with Company troops, was planned in Whitehall, not Leadenhall Street, and was timed to coincide with a successful attack on Havana, Cuba – which gives some idea of the global reach of European wars two centuries ago.

With the diwani in Bengal to protect, the Bengal army soon outgrew the smaller armies in Madras and Bombay. The Council in Bombay seemed to feel that their Presidency was a poor relation of the others, and embarked on an unwise spot of empire-building of its own. The first Mahratta war in 1779 ended ignominiously when the Bombay expeditionary force was harried from the field by the light, flexible Mahratta cavalry. To rub salt in the wounds, Hastings had had to send troops over from Bengal in belated support.

While the Directors of the Company could, with persuasion, see the justification for paying for permanent

Robert Clive, known to history as 'Clive of India' for his pivotal role in establishing the Company there.

infantry to defend their burgeoning Indian interests, they drew the line at cavalry, believing that superior artillery and small arms, combined with better-disciplined troops, would be ample to deal with any threat. The fact that man for man, cavalry cost twice as much as infantry would not have escaped the attention of the ever-parsimonious Directors, but officers in the field felt the lack of tactical flexibility. When the Company finally allowed cavalry they were able to attract the Muslim recruits who had previously somewhat eluded them, which had led to a religious imbalance in the armies and which was felt to be a source of potential problems. In the nineteenth century, cavalry, such as Skinner's Horse, was often irregular; this built on the traditional 'sillidar' system, whereby the troopers provided their own horse and equipment.

An additional complication in the command structure was added by the local contingents, which were under the control of the civilian rather than the military authorities in some states such as Gwalior and Hyderabad.

At its height, the Company's Indian army consisted of 250,000 men, of which no more than 45,000 were European officers and other ranks. There was no need to forcibly recruit sepoys; they were professional soldiers who served the Company in return for a livelihood, status, security and honour. A sepoy would often be a small landowner; the pay in the Company's service was sufficiently good for a man to be able to send home two thirds to support his family. He could also afford to employ a man to carry his bundle, and others to cook and look after him. Frequently of the Rajput warrior class or of high caste, he pursued the role that his social status required of him, and would require of his sons. Loyalty was a matter of caste honour, not engendered by any particular merit of the Company, whose officers were alien in culture, temperament and habits. Nonetheless, partly through the passage of time, partly as a result of the success of the Company in the field, and partly through the personalities of the officers, there did spring up a deeper loyalty, one which was abused during the time leading up to the Mutiny, and then fatally overestimated.

For European officers, the Indian army had many attractions. Unlike the Crown army, commissions were not bought but achieved on merit, which opened it to the ambitious sons of the middle classes. Nor, of course, could commissions be sold, so officers would try to make as much money as possible while on active service; the batta, or field allowances, were generous and exploited to the full, and

A sepoy of the Madras army photographed in 1852 and wearing a standard issue 'shako' helmet.

backhanders on supply and transport were the norm. Prize money and other bounty further supplemented the regular pay. Crown officers may have been contemptuous of the social standing of their counterparts in the Indian army, but their postings generally gave better opportunities to make substantial amounts of money, and the Company was a good paymaster. By 1796, regulations were enforced to give parity to Company and Crown officers, and to increase the number of European officers in the Company army. The

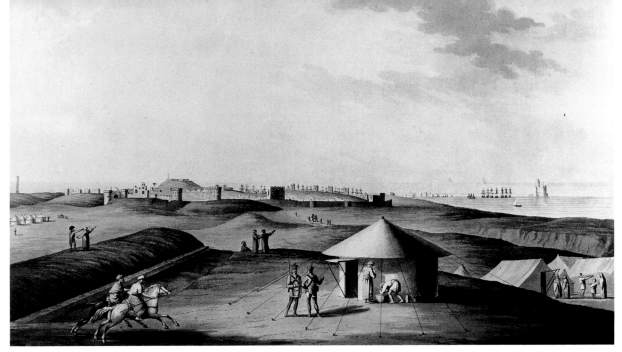

The Indian army pictured in 1801 at their camp in Alexandria, in Egypt.

latter had the effect of stifling the higher promotion prospects of the most able sepoys, and contributed to the background noise of disaffection at the time of the Mutiny. Training for this new European officer class was facilitated in 1809 by the founding of the Company's cadet college at Addiscombe in Surrey.

The Indian army was retained for the defence of India, but made a number of forays abroad in defence of that inter-est, marching across Egypt from the Red Sea in 1801 to take on Napoleon (who had already been beaten by another army marching from the Mediterranean), invading Java in 1811, and seeing action in Burma, China, Persia, Arabia and Afghanistan during the Company's Indian rule. By this time the sepoy battalions rivalled in effectiveness those of the Europeans, and the Bengal Commander-in-Chief boasted that some of his sepoy battalions '. . . would astonish the King of Prussia'.

The colourfully attired sepoys of the Bengal army, c. 1785.

Major Daniel Bamfield of the Bengal Native Infantry. He died in 1849 after the Battle of Chilianwalah.

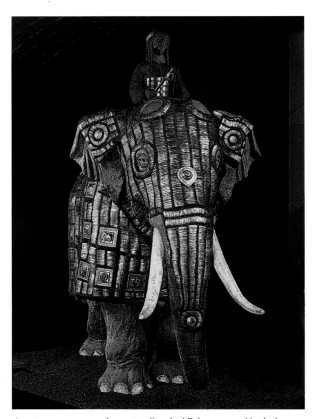

A unique, near-complete suit of early 17th-century Moghul elephant armour brought back to England from India by Clive.

RICHARD, BARON WELLESLEY

When Richard Wellesley, elder brother of the future Duke of Wellington was made Governor General in 1797, he amply exhibited a similar aptitude for war, pushing the frontiers of the Company's domains further and further into India on the basis that warlike states beyond the border required subduing, and once they were duly subdued, a new border was created with the next warlike state which thus required subduing, and so forth. The compelling logic of this strategy, called the 'Forward Policy', was successfully pursued, supported by a burgeoning nationalism at home, with politicians of all hues persuaded that the imposition of stability created the best conditions for social improvement in India. As a result of the disintegration of the Moghul Empire, India was dangerously unstable and culturally both used to, and equipped for, a state of more or less constant war; Wellesley chose to interpret that ever-volatile situation as a threat, and acted accordingly. He changed by force the Company's raj into a new empire, on a permanent war footing. The Directors might blanch at the expense, but the victories kept rolling in, and under Wellesley's administration, British rule became supreme.

ARMS AND ORDNANCE

Indian armies were unlike anything the English had encountered before. Their use of elephants as heavily-armoured animated tanks for battering down defences or charging through infantry was terrifying, but European weapon technology was consistently superior throughout the Company's 250-year presence in India, and was one of the key reasons for their successes in the field.

The Company established its own mills for making gunpowder in each of the Presidencies; with typically Anglocentric thinking, the Directors attempted to impose the standard English methods of manufacture, even when their experts told them that these methods

The Khan of Kelat and Sir Robert Sandeman conclude a treaty in 1867 which had been sought after since the Company's time.

were only necessary in damp northern climes, and that in India the sun provided a sure and swift way of drying the powder. Likewise, and perhaps with some justification, throughout its Indian adventure the Company sourced small arms in England, not trusting to Indian manufacture. In contrast to their frequent insensitivity to matters of caste and religion, the Company's officers made considerable efforts to adapt weapons to the slighter, smaller build of the sepoy, modifying standard British army designs, and continuing to supply the Indian cavalry with traditional curved sword blades long after they had become obsolete in the British army.

One simple innovation to the scabbard of the sword was made by Brigadier Sir John Jacob, commander of the Sind Irregular Horse. He created a wooden insert which prevented the blade of the sword becoming blunt through contact with the metal of the scabbard, and the practice was later adopted through the whole cavalry. He was a renowned officer, and attracted the best horsemen in India to his irregulars; this effectively prevented the incursion of Baluch bandits into the recently annexed province of Sind, and led eventually to Sandeman's treaty with local tribal chieftains (above). Sir John also invented a new type of rifle, with which he equipped two infantry regiments (Jacob's Rifles). The town he designed and built at Khangur in Sind was renamed Jacobabad after him.

General Sam Browne

General Sir Samuel James Browne, whose 14-bore percussion pistols are illustrated, was born in India, the son of a Company surgeon. He distinguished himself during the Mutiny, losing an arm in the process of capturing a gun single-handed. It used to be thought that his eponymous belt, which is still in use today, was the result of his attempts to deal with his disability, but in fact he invented it before he lost the arm.

William Hodson was the founder of his eponymous Irregular Horse, and had a spectacular career. He was the son of the canon of Lichfield, educated and widely read, but in the field a very demon; an expert swordsman who taunted opponents in battle, 'Come along now, make me sweat for it! Call yourself a swordsman? Try again, try again.' He eschewed the officer's sword, preferring to use the regular army weapon with its heavy hilt and leather grip – the officers' version had a fishskin grip. Although he had 'the fierce courage of a tiger unsubdued by any feelings of human compassion' his career ended in controversy with an unsubstantiated charge of fiddling the mess expenses, and the shooting of the king of Delhi's sons. He died at the relief of Lucknow in 1858.

THE TIGER AND THE LION: ENEMY AND FRIEND

The Company faced opponents of different kinds during its raj, defeating most by force of arms, allying itself with those who wished it and sometimes those who didn't, annexing, manipulating and politicking its way to power. The threats posed by the Tiger and the Lion to the Company typify on a grand scale the dramas played out on the stage of India.

Tipu, Sultan of Mysore was the most powerful threat to British hegemony in southern India in the late eighteenth century, and has become something of a protonationalist hero in modern India. He styled himself the 'Tiger of Mysore', and his insistence that tiger motifs were worked into his uniforms, cannons, cane handles, bed hangings, swords and thrones created a fine cult of tigerish personality, which may in part account for his remaining in the popular imagination of both India and Britain. His humiliating defeats of the English and his harsh treatment of prisoners during the Second Mysore War caused widespread hysteria in Britain, and Cornwallis's capture of Tipu's capital, Seringapatam, in the Third War was greeted with universal (English) acclaim. The treaty Cornwallis imposed on Tipu involved taking his two young sons hostage, as a guarantee of good behaviour. They were taken to Madras and looked after with exemplary kindness – treatment which inspired artists to patriotic

The rather fanciful rendition of the departure of Tipu Sultan's sons from the zenana by Thomas Stothard, c. 1800.

Tipu Sultan. Mysore's tiger in an unusually subdued mood.

Tipu's Tiger, one of the most popular exhibits at the Company's museum in Leadenhall Street.

A reverse view of Tipu's Tiger, showing the organ keyboard carved into its side.

flights of fancy in praise of Britain's 'benevolence and conquest'. In the Fourth Mysore War, which ended in 1799 with Tipu's final defeat and death (although his sons were once more led into captivity), the old enemy was finally laid to rest, with a similar outpouring of jingoistic fervour.

Stothard's painting (page 136) is a typical mishmash of misplaced sentiment and inaccuracy, involving characters from the second event depicted as if in the first, and the presence of strange men in the zenana (women's quarters), which would never have been countenanced. Yet it does capture beautifully the self-image of the British as stern but fair administrators of justice, and the exotic defencelessness of Indian women (despite their Empire clothes . . .). Tipu remained a compelling theme, and, long after the event, in 1839 the discovery of his body after the battle was depicted in suitably grand style by Sir David Wilkie.

Ranjit Singh, the Maharajah of Lahore and wily lion of the Punjab.

Tipu's 'Man-Tyger-Organ' captures one aspect of his character, his macabre but childlike cruelty, and is his most popular legacy. Constructed by French craftsmen, it depicts the true story of the death of the son of a Company general, Sir Hector Monroe, trapped under a tiger; when the handle is turned, the soldier screams and the tiger roars. Should that not prove sufficiently amusing, there is a small organ inside for playing tiger ragas. Captured at Seringapatam, it was exhibited in pride of place in the Company's museum, then at the Great Exhibition, and is now in the Nehru Gallery of the Victoria and Albert Museum, which inherited many of its Indian exhibits from the Company.

One of the ironies of the Company's war against Tipu is that in many ways Tipu had accomplished in Mysore what the Company later aspired to achieve in India as a whole. Having inherited the state from his father, the General Hyder Ali, he had modernised the administration, improved the infrastructure through road and irrigation projects, had developed agriculture and encouraged new industries, such as silk cultivation. As a Muslim in a predominantly Hindu state, Tipu practised a high degree of religious tolerance, and, through his tiger cult, was an avid patron of the arts. He was esteemed

by those he ruled over, and his armies were fiercely effective, and loyal. If he had been an ally of the Company, he would have been admired publicly by those who recognised his abilities in private, but he had vowed to remove the Company from India, and that, when it came down to it, was all that mattered. However, when it comes to his credibility as a prototype nationalist hero, against his implacable hatred of the English must be set the fact that his father had usurped the Mysore throne from an Hindu incumbent, who, ironically, it took the Company to restore, albeit on a short leash.

Ranjit Singh, Maharajah of Lahore, on the other hand, allowed the British to dub him the 'Lion of the Punjab', and although he cut a less dashing figure than Tipu, being partially paralysed and pitted with smallpox, he left a more lasting legacy in the shape of the Sikh control of the Indian Punjab, a long shadow of which remains to this day. Sikhism was founded by Guru Nanak in the late fifteenth century, in an endeavour to unite Muslim and Hindu in a benevolent and undogmatic religion. Instead, it first became a revolutionary movement in defence of its freedom of worship, especially when threatened by the intolerant Moghul Emperor Aurangzeb, and later was riven by factionalism. Son of a Sikh leader, by the age of seventeen Ranjit Singh had already managed to secure Lahore for his followers, and was quickly to turn the brigand bands of rival Sikhs into a coherent unit that quickly expanded their territories. By the age of twenty-five, in 1805, only the Company, which had taken Delhi from the remains of the Moghul Empire, stood in the way of his domination of northern India. In contrast to Tipu, Ranjit Singh chose to treat with, rather than fight the English, ceding new conquests to the Company in return for formal agreement of the borders of his Punjab territories.

In person, Ranjit Singh was a mass of contradictions: austere of dress, his Court was splendid; a skilled warrior, he was addicted to alcohol, ground pearls, debauchery and hypochondria; regarded in Company circles as avaricious and untrustworthy, he nonetheless managed to maintain their support, helped by his charming and gentle manner. He encouraged trade and agriculture within the Punjab, and reformed the revenue system, as well as founding the great Sikh temples. Upon his death in 1838 his four wives and seven concubines threw themselves, voluntarily it is said, upon his funeral pyre, but his successor could not maintain the modus vivendi Ranjit Singh had established with the Company, and within eleven years it had annexed the Punjab.

Tipu's mausoleum at Seringapatam, photographed in the late 1850s. His father and mother are buried alongside him.

THE BLACK HOLE OF CALCUTTA

While the fighting and factionalism which bedevilled the Madras Presidency showed no signs of diminishing, Company traders in Calcutta were enjoying a period of relative peace and prosperity. That changed with the death of Nawab Alivardi, Khan of Bengal in 1756. His heir, Siraj-ud-dualah, had heeded the lessons of South India well, and was determined to prevent Europeans from gaining a secure foothold in Bengal. He ordered that both the Company and the French should stop fortifying their settlements. The French complied; the English did not, so the Nawab destroyed the newly-built defences for them, and captured a number of Europeans.

The so-called Black Hole of Calcutta became the historical catalyst that conveniently elevated the Company's military response to that of a mission of holy revenge, but the deaths of Englishmen in captivity at the hands of Siraj-ud-dualah were most probably unpremeditated and the horrors greatly exaggerated by the only chronicler of the disaster, J Holwell, a member of the Calcutta Council, who decided to give a starring role in the tragedy to one J Holwell. His gripping description of a tiny, airless room, stifling temperatures, crushed bodies and gruesome suffocation has an enduring gothic appeal, but one Indian historian has been so churlish as

Company troops in Rangoon during the successful prosecution of the First Burmese War in 1825.

to suggest that, instead of one hundred and forty six Europeans being led into the Hole, of whom only twenty-three emerged alive next morning, nine went in and six came out, three having died from wounds previously received.

For the English in Empire years, the myth of the Black Hole conveniently encapsulated the idea of both the depraved brutality of the Indian ruler and the righteousness of those who punished him, and the massacre was widely taught as reported truth in English schools. For Indian historians, it encapsulated perfidious Albion and the overweening arrogance of power. In either case its symbolic vitality long outlasted its basis in historical truth, and the fact that the melodramatic name, the 'Black Hole', has been

A Birman war boat. These presented little threat to the Company's ships in the Burmese Wars.

appropriated by astronomers to describe a particularly inescapable feature of the cosmos seems an apt reflection of its likely future role on the historical stage.

CLIVE AND PLASSEY

To avenge the defeat at Calcutta, reinforcements were swiftly dispatched from Madras, with General Clive leading the land forces and Admiral Watson the navy. By early 1757, Calcutta was back in Company hands, and any chance of a French strike pre-empted by the capture of their settlement at Chandernagar. Clive moved swiftly to consolidate the Company's position by conspiring with a powerful commander and the wealthiest banker in Bengal to overthrow Siraj-ud-dualah.

Like a fixed wrestling bout, the outcome of the Battle of Plassey was predetermined by the backroom deals struck by Clive, and the great victory was no more than a sham, enabling the Company to replace the redundant Nawab with their placeman, his former finance minister, Mir Jafar. The successful outcome cast the Company in the role of kingmaker, and their effortless overthrow of Mir Jafar when he had outlived his usefulness, in 1760, confirmed them in this all-powerful role. With the Company shifting status from that of besieged traders to the power behind the throne in a matter of months, no wonder Clive was seduced by the possibilities that lay ahead.

In 1764, Clive decided to negotiate a new basis for the Company's operations in Bengal, and accepted the diwani from the Moghul Emperor, Shah Alam. The diwani gave the Company the right to collect the revenues of Bengal, and thus effectively to govern the state. In return, the Company paid the emperor a fee, while the rest of the system functioned on its usual Indian basis. In this respect the Company was merely a substitute for the Nawab of Bengal, who had collected the revenues and paid tribute in like fashion.

Clive personified the aggrandising, aggressive force which was by now associated with the Company, and which, to the extent that the Company succeeded beyond its wildest dreams, was due in great part to Clive. In fact, Clive envisaged a role far beyond those wildest dreams, and as early as 1759 was hinting in secret correspondence with Pitt the Elder that an active imperial status could readily be achieved: the revenues were available to fund a kingdom, but 'so large a sovereignty . . . [is] too extensive for a mercantile company'. Clive's machinations were fundamentally subversive to the Company's interests and presaged the Crown's intervention in Company affairs, instigated by Lord North's Regulating Act in 1773, and which signalled the end of Company autonomy, and its eventual absorption by the Crown in 1858.

BURMESE INTRIGUES

Knowing little about the Company, except from Armenian and Muslim traders who generally had nothing good to say about them, King Bodawpaya (who ruled Burma 1782-1819) sent embassies to India, seeking an alliance with anyone – Moghul, French, Mahratta – against the English. Initially, they came in the guise of pilgrims to Benares, Lahore and even Peshawar; when the English discovered the true nature of their missions, they sent them back. Some found their way to Delhi in 1820, where they were painted at the instigation of William Fraser (see page 92). As Buddhists, they collected a number of sacred books and relics, and even took Hindu girls back to Burma as presents to the King – daughters, they told him, of suppliant Indian rulers.

The Company declared war in 1824. The Indian-Burmese border was, as they saw it, insufficiently defined and the Burmese showed no inclination to define it. The war cost £13,000,000 and the lives of 20,000 soldiers from

The improbable Hairy Family from Mandalay, an ethnological discovery of the Burmese campaign.

both sides, and very nearly ended in disaster in the sweltering reaches of the Irrawaddy beyond Rangoon. But the Company emerged from the eventual treaty with substantial gains, including Assam, the future tea-growing centre of India, and increased the security of the coast nearly all the way to Penang.

The Second Burmese War (1852-3) was a grand-scale punitive raid designed to bring the Burmese to heel – they had treated the Company's officials in the capital, Ava, with a lack of proper respect, it was thought, and 'an insult offered to the British flag at the mouth of the Ganges should be resented as promptly and as fully as an insult offered at the mouth of the Thames'. Resentment was expressed in this case by a small army which captured Rangoon and annexed Pegu province and the entire coastline. At the bargain price of less than a £1,000,000, the Company now held the coast of the Indian Ocean from Singapore to the mouth of the Indus.

COMPANY GOES WEST

> *'It is the business of government to open and secure the roads for the merchant.'*
>
> Lord Palmerston.

THE NORTH AMERICAN CONNECTION

Although its Charter only gave the East India Company a monopoly on trade to the east of the Cape of Good Hope, the sheer scale of its enterprise gave it significant influence on the newly emerging American colonies. The nineteenth-century American historian Henry Newton Stevens maintained that the *Mayflower* which participated in the Third Voyage of the Company was the same ship that was later to take the Pilgrim Fathers on their voyage from Plymouth and, thirty years later, to sink off Masulipatam. He was later shown to be mistaken, but the fact remains that the burgeoning colonial world, and the companies that served it, were all interconnected.

In the early days of the seventeenth century the small circle of influential merchants in the City of London which formed the Company in 1600 had its fingers in a number of other trading pies. The Governor of the East India Company in its first decade, Sir Thomas Smyth, was also the first Governor of the Virginia Company, founded in 1606, the first British colonial enterprise in North America. Both Companies shared headquarters in Smyth's house, together with the Levant Company.

Thwarted in their search for a Northwest passage to the Indies over the top of North America (see page 14) and forced to share the sea-lanes with the Portuguese on the more conventional route to China and the Spice Islands, the Company had little contact with America until it success-

'Boston boys' empty the Company tea chests into the sea. The Boston Tea Party, as depicted by Edward Gooch in 1775.

CHAPTER XIII

THE EAST INDIA COMPANY

fully established its trade in India; then private traders or interlopers based in New England began causing headaches and, as the Company saw it at least, interfering with their monopoly.

The American brothers Elihu and Thomas Yale forged notable careers for themselves in the Company's service. Elihu rose to become Governor of Madras, and from there, in 1689, he sent Thomas on what was the Company's first direct trading mission to China, paving the way for the opening up of that country to the Company's traders. His brother was later disgraced, but Elihu returned to America with the fortune that he had earned in India, donating part of it to his old school which, in gratitude, renamed itself 'Yale College' in 1718. St Mary's, in Madras, the oldest English church on the subcontinent, was an earlier beneficiary of Yale's largesse.

The East India Company brought new goods and fashions to Europe, but North America was never far behind. The light cottons of India were well suited to the humid summers of the south-eastern states, and calicoes, chintzes, silks, spices, coffee, cocoa and Chinese earthenware as well as tea all found their way across the water, mainly shipped by private traders from the Company's warehouses in London, since the Company's Charter did not allow it to re-export goods itself. Textiles, tea and ironware became the most important British exports to America. Even after American Independence, the East India Company remained a highly competitive importer of goods into the United States, resulting in occasional flare-ups, such as the trade war of 1812-1814.

THE BOSTON TEA PARTY

Tea had been popular on the northeastern seaboard of America since the 1650s — indeed, it is likely that it was a well-established favourite with the Dutch burghers of New Amsterdam before it became widely known in England — and after the city became New York in 1674, tea gardens modelled on those of London's Vauxhall and Ranelagh flourished on Manhattan island. By the 1760s, America was importing over a million pounds of the beverage a year — most of it smuggled — to avoid the punitive duties imposed by the Crown even on re-exported tea. After 1767, merchants could 'drawback' the full amount of duty paid on the tea, and the result was that smuggling was almost completely eradicated.

However, taxation issues between the Government and the American colonies were at the time a political hot potato, and when a new tea tax was imposed, the revenues from which were to go to paying the salaries of British officials, protests broke out. New Englanders were exhorted to give up tea in favour of a root from Labrador with 'a very physical taste':

Throw aside your Bohea and your Green Hyson Tea
And all things with a new-fangled duty.
Procure a good store of the choice Labradore,
For there'll soon be enough here to suit ye.
(Quoted in B W Larabee, The Boston Tea Party,
New York, OUP, 1964)

There was no sudden demand for 'Labradore', but legitimate tea sales plummeted to only a hundred thousand pounds in 1770, and smuggling thrived again. At that time the East India Company was not only in debt, but had also built up substantial stocks (twenty-one million pounds) of tea in London; it persuaded the Government to draft the Tea Act of 1773, allowing them to sell tea in America at a price that included the duties which the Company, but not the colonists, could drawback. As a result of political horse-trading, the Bill was passed on the nod. 'No Bill of such momentous consequences ever received so little attention on its passage through Parliament' (B W Larabee, ibid.). With the Company dumping their vast surplus on the Americans at cheap prices, legitimate traders as well as smugglers were threatened.

The Company had trouble finding exporters willing to involve themselves in this dubious enterprise, and eventually the tea had to be shipped on the Company's account, but not in EastIndiamen. The ships with the first consignment berthed at Griffin's Wharf, Boston, where, on 16 December 1773, the tea chests were unceremoniously emptied into the sea by patriots dressed as native American Indians, their true identities concealed by blankets and lampblack. As the average weight of a full tea chest at the time was 450 pounds, this was an heroic feat in every sense of the word. The operation involved members of an 'irregular' Freemason's Lodge which met in an upstairs room of the Green Dragon coffee house. Two of them, Warren and Paul Revere, sat on the Lodge's Committee of

The Western Hemisphere, with its virtually impregnable Northern passages.

The Stars and Stripes

The story of the origin of the Stars and Stripes, the American flag, forms an essential part of every schoolchild's education in the United States, but, predictably, sentiment fatally allied to patriotism has overtaken fact. Vexillologists (flag experts) have waged learned war with historians about the origins of Betsy Ross's supposed gift to George Washington of the Union Flag with its thirteen stripes and thirteen stars representing the schismatic states of the new Union. As yet unrecognised, and of great potential interest to those who espouse the Freemasonic conspiracy theory about the origins of the American Revolution, is the fact that the flag of the East India Company had since about 1660 also contained thirteen alternating red and white stripes, with the top left quartile, like the present day Stars and Stripes, reserved for, initially the cross of St George and, later, the Union Jack. Why the designer of the Company flag should have chosen thirteen stripes is as yet unclear, but the association of that number with the Last Supper, the lunar months, and the minor trumps of the Tarot is irresistible. A strong candidate for the designer of the first Union flag is Francis Hopkinson, a delegate from New Jersey to the Continental Congress for 'Currency design, design for the great seal of the U.S., a treasury seal, a design for the flag . . . '. The use of Masonic motifs in the currency and seals of the United States is well documented, but the link of the Company's flag to that prevailing symbolism of the newly formed Union is as yet unexplored. Even now, the Stars and Stripes retains thirteen alternating red and white stripes, although, perhaps significantly, in the opposite sequence to the Company Flag of the time of the American Revolution. Vexillologists have more work to do, and the full extent of the Company's contrapunctal connections with the cause of American Independence may yet be revealed . . .

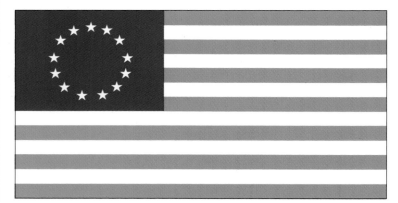

The East India Company ensign
1707 – 1801.

The Stars and Stripes of the
Union, 1777

Correspondence which co-ordinated revolutionary patriotic acts between the American cities. As we have seen, the Company's own Committee of Correspondence was a crucial element in its management structure and administration from the early days, and it is tempting to think that the name had been adopted by the American patriots as an ironic gesture of contempt for the hated British and the Company's teas.

Further shipments were also destroyed at Charleston, Philadelphia, New York and a second time at Boston, but is the Boston Tea Party that has lived on in American folklore. Nevertheless, and contrary to expectations, by the early 1800s the East India Company was back in business selling tea to North America – though to an America that was by now independent of British rule: General Cornwallis's defeat at Yorktown, Virginia, in 1781 had proved to be Britain's last defence of the colony. Cornwallis himself had disapproved of Britain's taxation laws in America but was later to serve with great distinction in the Company's service in India; it was said of him that while he lost a colony in the West, he won one in the East.

General Cornwallis revives his career after his humiliations in America by receiving the sons of Tipu as hostage.

VANCOUVER AND THE FUR TRADE

The Company's monopoly, officially chartered to include everything east of the Cape of Good Hope, was vaguely understood to end, if anywhere, in the Philippines. In the late eighteenth century the Company was constantly looking for ways to earn the silver bullion it needed to pay for the prodigious quantities of China tea that it was shipping, and when it became apparent that there was a good market for furs in China, they naturally applied themselves to the getting of furs. Fortunately, William Dalrymple, the Company's hydrographer, had a keen commercial eye, and was swift to suggest that Alaskan furs, especially those of the much sought-after sea otter, were readily available information that he had acquired from a published report of the last voyage of Captain Cook. John Savage, in the service of the Company in Madras, had spotted the same information, and, with the blessing of the Company, two ships under his command left Bombay in 1785 for the North Pacific. Unknown to them, a similar expedition set up by the newly established Bengal Fur Society, left Calcutta two months later. The Company in India did not fund these ventures, but was well aware of their purpose and potential; it also neglected to inform London.

The two expeditions met, to their mutual surprise and resentment, in Prince William Sound, Alaska. It says much for the enterprising spirit of the times that two English naval commanders, inspired by the same report, charged with the same mission, both with the covert blessing of the East India Company's Indian operation could meet for the first time in a virtually unexplored corner of the American Northwest. Savage promptly headed off with his pelts for Canton in high dudgeon, while the other commander, John Meares, rashly decided to winter where he was. Only ten of his crew of thirty-one were left by the time the pack ice had receded, and then another English ship, the *Queen Charlotte*, sailed into the cove, having made the voyage west from London around the Cape of Good Hope. Its captain, George Dixon, was employed by the recently formed King George Sound Company, set up with the authorisation of the Government in response, inevitably, to the report of Cook's voyage. Meares recognised the superiority of his rival's claim, and set off for Canton, followed closely by Dixon, where the pelts fetched excellent prices. Although the Bengal Fur Company subsequently disappeared, a joint venture between the various parties flourished for a further ten years, when the trade was halted by the actions of the Spanish, who exerted their claim over the entire west coast of America, capturing three vessels under Meares' command. The East India Company appears thereafter to have given due consideration to the definition of 'east', and was not seen on the west coast of America again.

J.Webber del.

A View of SNUG CORNER

W. Ellis s

, in PRINCE WILLIAM's SOUND.

COMPANY AT WORK, REST AND PLAY

'England, when once of peace and wealth possest
Began to think frugality a jest,
So grew polite: hence all her well-bred heirs
Gamesters and jockies turn'd, and cricket play'rs.'

Soame Jenyns

THE CANTONMENT AND THE CLUB

War became more or less a way of life for the English in India; the very situation of a tiny European population holding sway over millions demanded that it should be so. The cantonment lay at the hub of that martial society. Laid out in an orderly grid a few miles from the centre of the town which it dominated, the cantonment was mainly a barracks, but also partly a European enclave, provided with church, shops, and the club.

The club in the East came to symbolise the insularity of the English; cocooned from native mayhem, a gentleman (and, in some rooms, a woman) could read reports of the latest campaign, drink punch silently served by an uniformed bearer and exchange murmured approval of the new Collector, all in an atmosphere of ordered tranquillity. The bar, bridge and billiards provided entertainment; the walls and watchmen provided security; and for a while at least it was possible to believe oneself back in St James.

The grandest clubs in India were found, naturally, in the Presidencies – the Old Madras Club, purpose-built in the preferred classical style, and the Bengal Club in Calcutta, which took over two vast town houses – and reflected the ambitions of their members. Their exclusion of native members or guests was an expression of the separation of the ruler and the ruled which characterised the Company in the run up to the Mutiny. Further from the laissez-faire interaction of a nautch party or a cockfight one could not get.

'Chasing a Tiger across a River' from 'Oriental Field Sports', the Indian hunting man's bible.

CHAPTER XIV

THE MEMSAHIB

'The respectful designation of a European married lady in the Bengal Presidency' (*Hobson-Jobson*).

A creature of caricature and historical complexity, the memsahib has become the personification of all that was best and worst of the Company's raj. Accused, *inter alia*, of having created singlehanded the missionary's inflexible position, the alienation of the loyal sepoy, a deep vat of racial prejudice, the emasculation of her menfolk, and, as a final flourish, the Mutiny itself, she now has no shortage of apologists in the ranks of post-feminist historians, who identify in her the nascent struggle. How she laboured under Tennyson's description, 'the soft and milky rabble of womankind'; how she choked at her depiction in propaganda paintings resignedly commending her soul to Christ as the lust-crazed natives burst into her last refuge (one ample shoulder exposed, as if inviting ravishment); how she suffocated in the conventional air of this exclusive man's world . . . but history has not yet done with the memsahib.

Contemporary accounts frequently paint an unsympathetic picture: ' . . . she falls victim to indolent habits and coarse convictions – the sylph-like form which distinguished the youth of her arrival is rapidly exchanged for an exterior of which obesity and swarthiness are prominent, and the bottle and the hookah become frequent and offensive companions'. (An Old Resident, *Real Life in India*, London 1847). In the meantime she waits stoically for months to visit the dentist, changes her clothes four times a day; fries by day and suffocates by night; wears dresses more suited to Ascot in spring, and watches them moulder in the monsoon; driven to distraction by the brain-fever bird, she catches a fever herself, anticipates her imminent demise and frets about what will happen to the children; takes tea with a friend one day and buries her the next; gives birth in the company of a drunken midwife, then nurses the infant in the back of an ammunition cart during a siege. In short, this (composite) memsahib endured what no woman back home had to endure, and received scant recognition for it.

The memsahib was of course a stereotype, but exceptions tended to be exceptional. One of the rare women to make a career in India, Emma Roberts, was a writer and journalist with outspoken views on racism, and editor of The *Oriental Observer* in Calcutta between 1828 and 1832. Whilst women like Isabella Fane, daughter of an army commander, sneered in her letters home at the 'blackees' and the pretensions of Indian aristocrats, Emily Eden, sister of Governor General Lord Auckland, observes shrewdly of Delhi: '. . . a suggestive and moralising place – such stupendous remains of power and wealth passed and passing away – and somehow I feel we horrid English have just "gone and done it", merchandised it, revenued it, and spoiled it all. I am not very fond of Englishmen out of their own country' (ed. Eleanor Eden, *Letters from India*, London 1872).

Perhaps the best that could be said was that the memsahib came equipped with the ordinary narrow-minded views of her time, and, in the face of the vast, mysterious, frightening subcontinent, hung on to them for dear life. Or, less charitably, 'They were sent out as portable little packets of morality, to comfort their men, keep the bloodline clean, and remind them of their mothers' (Jane Robinson, *Angels of Albion*, Penguin 1997).

FOOD

It is natural to assume that the early Company servants in India were faced with profoundly different cuisine from the one they were used to. However, spices had become commonplace in Europe as a result of the activities of the Portuguese during the previous century, so that the recipe for a 'dumpoked' fowl served in Surat by Muslims to their English guests was almost exactly the same as that for an English chicken pie in 1615, with its currants, raisins, cinnamon and mace. In England, as in India, hands or bread were used for eating – the use of forks was not yet common – and where pan was chewed in India as a digestif, the English chewed voidee, a similar spicy concoction. In those early days, Indian cuisine itself was not as we know it today. Baked or boiled lamb and game meat, and fish from the seas or rivers, were widely consumed – familiar fare to the English – whilst chilli had only been introduced from the West Indies by the Portuguese a century earlier (where it was used it was known as the Goan pepper). Cashews, tomatoes, papayas and pineapple were likewise recent additions to Indian cuisine.

The factors at Surat, for example, might be isolated and fearful of disease, but at least they could face the day with a full stomach. A small breakfast of 'burnt wine' (made hot with spices) was followed by lunch, the main meal of the day; a typical Sunday feast might include deer, antelope, hare, partridge, pilau rice, pistachios, plums and apricots. And, of course, copious quantities of drink. A large lunch made a hard-working afternoon unlikely, and over the next two hundred years the main meal of the day gradually migrated towards the evening, with the place of lunch taken by 'tiffin', a supposedly light snack which could frequently consist of several meat curries accompanied by beer or Madeira.

Since most of the commercial trade of the Company was carried on ships returning home, freight charges for the outward voyage of EastIndiamen were reasonable. From the earliest times the Company had supplied European alcohol for its factory messes, and servants would try to recreate the feel of a European dinner; John MacDonald (*Memoirs of an 18th Century Footman*, Century, 1985) prided himself on the meals that he created for his master in Bombay, which included 'two silver *épargnes* full of sweetmeats, and three crystal stands with syllabubs and jellies, in a row in the middle of the table, with three rows of plates with fruits and deserts from top to bottom . . . the black men admired it, and said, "Your table looks like a diamond, Steward". . .' Later, European food became widely available: '. . . the dinner just like an English one, for what could not be procured in India was brought from Europe; including hermetically sealed fruits, fish, and meats, and preserves, with champagne, etc' (Ruth Coopland, *A Lady's Escape from Gwalior*, London, 1859). The invention of tinning in England in 1818 was soon appreciated in India; in Simla in the 1830s it was possible to find tinned truffled hare pâté from the Périgord.

The more active men and women in India rose at about five o'clock to go riding before the heat of the day set in, and took chota hazri of tea and biscuits at six. A more substantial breakfast was eaten at about ten o'clock, consisting of chops, devilled kidneys, stews, hashes and brains. Kedgeree, found on the breakfast sideboard of every country house party until recent times, derived from 'khicari', a spiced mixture of lentils and rice. It was adopted, and adapted, by the English, who took the idea home with them in the eighteenth century. Out went the lentils and in came smoked haddock, chopped eggs, onions and parsley; only the rice remains of the original. Curry was also a feature of the Indian breakfast table, and curries were served for breakfast on EastIndiamen from the eighteenth century onwards – a practice that was adopted by the merchant navy in the East.

Taylor's Emporium, a leading Calcutta store. Only the distant dhotis betray its Indian home.

Whether in the army, trade or civil service, much of a Company servant's time in India was spent on the move – the vast distances and poor communications ensured that. There were always plenty of servants to handle the logistical problems of food – one Collector considered it inconceivable to travel with fewer than sixty servants and eighty porters to look after him. Cows could be driven in advance to each prospective camp to supply fresh milk, and a swaying camel made an ideal butter churn. An antecedent of the pressure cooker – the so-called 'pepper pot' – was indispensable. A substantial meat and vegetable stew, suitably spiced, could be cooked up in advance and reheated at each stop. Fresh food supplies could be prevented from sweating in the heat by carrying them in a wicker basket; the squarish hamper with an opening top lid had become very popular in England by the early nineteenth century for picnics.

There was no officers' mess for the army on the move until after 1808. Before that, officers would take turns to invite all their colleagues to dinner, supplying both food and wine. The foot soldiers were kept supplied by the legions of camp followers who turned an overnight camp into a veritable bazaar. Food supply concessions were one of the ways in which a senior Company officer could make money on the side. Clive, whose idea of a mere perquisite was another man's idea of a fortune, is estimated to have made £40,000 by supplying lamb to the army.

The name for the most famous sauce in the world, ketchup, comes from the Chinese 'koetsiap', a brine of pickled fish to which the eighteenth-century English added tomatoes for good measure. A close second in the sauce hall of fame is Worcestershire Sauce, which owes its existence to Lord Sandys, Governor of Bengal at the start of the nineteenth century. Returning to England on leave, he asked his local chemist to make up his favourite recipe for a relish, provided by his Indian cook. Some was also stored in a stone jar against his lordship's return, and three years later it had matured in a most interesting way; soon Lea and Perrins' Worcestershire Sauce hit the market. The recipe has remained practically the same for over a hundred and fifty years – onions, shallots, garlic, chillis, anchovies, tamarind, cloves, molasses and vinegar, though soya had to be dropped when supplies dried up in the Second World War and has never found its way back. Worcestershire Sauce could even be found commercially in India by the end of the nineteenth century.

The Hindi word 'catni' was applied across a broad range of condiments and entered the English language as chutney. Chutneys were used by the English in India from the start of their time there.

MANNERS, PROTOCOL AND PRECEDENCE

The Company's servants in India were not renowned for the sophistication of their manners. Three councillors sent out to Bengal were astonished by what they found: 'They [the councillors] hated the British because of their bad manners and infantile pursuits; skill at putting out a candle with a well thrown bread pellet was considered a social achievement of the highest order' (Quoted in M Edwardes, *The Nabob at Home*, Constable, London 1991). Bread throwing was also seen as permissible sport for a lady, and only stopped in the Bengal Presidency when it resulted in a near-fatal duel.

In other respects, petty protocol was strictly observed. Who should lead whom into dinner, and who sat next to whom, was a matter of great debate, particularly in the mofussil where entertainment had to be gleaned from all the minutiae of life. If umbrage could possibly be taken, it

surely would be; one lady whose husband had recently been knighted was outraged by the precedence given at a Governor's dinner to another lady whose husband had also been knighted. She commented sympathetically to him on how difficult it must be to know how to place people at table. 'Not at all,' he replied. 'You see, the people who matter don't mind, and the people who mind don't matter.'

SERVANTS

The sheer multiplicity of servants was bewildering. The very poorest European would have at least two, and at the other end of the scale the numbers could reach hundreds – the Governor General was followed by a flotilla of four hundred staff if he went for a weekend to his Calcutta country retreat in his leather-lined, marble-bathroomed barge. To have one hundred servants was not considered extraordinary, and such vital tasks as keeping the master's hookah filled might be one man's sole responsibility.

The caste role of each servant was strictly defined, and the necessity of understanding this hierarchy could frequently be frustrating. Pictured with a calm and collected Lady Impey in her boudoir is her munshi (interpreter), a boy to fan her, standing behind, and a milliner delivering a new hat in front; others are (anti-clockwise from the millner): her European butler; the steward; a door-keeper and usher; two thread twisters (seated); a durzi (tailor); a mali (gardener); two more tailors; a chuprassi (messenger); another door-keeper and another usher and two embroiderers. Although her husband was a senior judge in Calcutta, there is nothing unusual about this busy household throng except the European butler. Converted Christians, contrary to expectations, were said to make the most untrustworthy servants; having taken their master's religion, they saw no reason to baulk at his worldly goods, too.

The ubiquity of servants contributed to the indolence to which memsahibs were particularly prone: 'The real Indian ladies lie on a sofa, and, if they drop their handkerchiefs, they just lower their voices and say "Boy!" in a very gentle tone, and then creeps in, perhaps, some old wizened, skinny brownie, looking like a superannuated thread-paper' (Julia Maitland, 1843). The running of the household was the responsibility of the khansamar (or dubash in the south)

Lady Impey's boudoir with the servants in attendance.

who would go to market but would never carry anything home himself. He was expected to take a commission on purchases (the dastur) of about five per cent; less worldly-wise employers would see this as cheating, and in vain try to circumvent it. Europeans tended to view Indian servants as children, prone to lying and cheating, but often it was the result of a failure to understand a different system.

For exceptional items such as clothes, which the khansamar could not be expected to buy, the memsahib could visit the shops that sprang up in the Presidencies; by 1800, there were thirty such in Calcutta. The latest Paris fashions could be studied in year-old magazines, and clothes of new arrivals were subject to keen scrutiny. The tailor could then be asked to make clothes up to order. In the mofussil, box-wallahs would visit the house carrying their wares with them.

Although of low status among her compatriots, the ayah or nursemaid was generally well paid and well treated. The dangers of employing a bad nurse ran to more than the obvious; she might take to eating chilli before breast-feeding the memsahib's pride and joy, or worse, opium: in some cases, unscrupulous ayahs were known to feed their charges grains of opium directly to ensure that they slept.

Although the Company was not actively involved in the slave trade, and banned slavery in the so-called independent states of India in 1842, the treatment of servants was far from exemplary. Elihu Yale, the future governor of Madras, was so incensed when his butler left without giving proper notice that he fabricated a charge of piracy against him, and the man was duly hanged. Beatings, kickings and verbal abuse were all too frequent, and it was the exceptional employer who treated his servants with respect. Servants were expected to provide references. But these often came from employers long-departed from the district, or from this life entirely, or were forged by the local letter-writer, who might extol the imaginary virtues of the potential employee. Indeed, this practice continues to this day; a clerk seeking employment was recently recommended as 'prayerful and dictionarised'.

For European men recently arrived in India, the linch-pin employee was the banyan – an agent or facotum who would find him a house, horses, servants, etc. Once the master was established, the banyan became a vital go-between in all commercial transactions, and could make a substantial fortune for himself: some of the great trading dynasties of India were founded in this way. Banyans invested time, effort and money in nurturing their relationship with their employer, and if the employer inconsiderately chose to die within a couple of years of arrival, the banyan might well find himself out of pocket.

INDOOR PURSUITS

Chess was invented in India in the sixth century AD, and the game spread to China and Europe. Special 'Company' sets were commissioned from local ivory craftsmen, featuring the Company soldiers in white, and those of the Maharaja stained red: such sets are rare now, and much sought after by collectors.

Playing cards based on mythological themes were known in pre-Moghul India, and the first Europeans brought their own cards and games with them. Bridge became, and remains, one of the most popular games, especially among the higher classes in India. Backgammon, originating in Persia, was popular in India before the arrival of the British, but was quickly adopted by them: 'Our evening amusements instead of your stupid Harmonics, was playing cards and backgammon, chewing beetle and smoking cheroots' (Old Country Captain, *Indian Gazette*, 1781).

HUNTING, RIDING AND HORSE RACING

Hunting and its associated sports, hawking and archery, were favourite pastimes in pre-European India. The Moghul method of driving game into a circular corral – either a stockade or a circle of people – was adopted enthusiastically by the British, who came to see the tiger as the most prestigious prey; a tiger skin on the floor of an English mansion was a sure sign of an Indian connection. Tiger hunting was frequently conducted from the back of an elephant, which afforded some measure of protection.

The Moghuls used to hunt carnivorous game with a spear as a test of princely manhood. In a debased form, this became the ubiquitous pig-sticking of the mofussil – a perilous sport, which evolved from hurling spears from horseback at passing wild boars to something not unlike jousting, with a lance firmly gripped beneath the arm. By the early nineteenth century, there was sufficient interest in hunting in India for the publication of a series of prints which depicted the variety of prey and the methods of hunting them down.

A spectacular pawn from a Company chess set. Being a white piece, the elephant is ridden by a sahib and his wife.

Tiger hunting from the relative safety of the back of an elephant. From 'Oriental Field Sports'.

The Prince's first tiger. Edward, the future Emperor of India, sits top left.

The traditional English sport of hunting to hounds was transposed to India, with the uneatable represented by the jackal and the unspeakable by sahibs galloping across the countryside with imported packs of hounds. As happened with the Army of the Indus when it invaded Afghanistan, these packs would sometimes be taken on campaign for the amusement of the officers.

Racing, and its associated gambling, was the preferred leisure occupation of the English of the time, and the Company lost no time in establishing race courses throughout the East wherever there was a sufficient European population to support it. The breeding and acquisition of good horses was as important then as today. John MacDonald notes: 'Mr Mathison bought the famous horse Chillabie from Macao (to Bombay), at this time four years old; he was chained in Colonel Keating's stable by the head and legs. He had killed an Arab at Macao and on the passage had almost killed another' (*Memoirs of an 18th Century Footman*, Century, 1985).

The grandstand at the Madras racecourse doubled as the Assembly Rooms: 'The Race Ground is between seven and eight miles from Madras, and near St Thomas's mount which, in this view, appears to the right of the Assembly Rooms. The races are supported by English gentlemen resident in Madras, and its neighbourhood. The amusement takes place in the cool season, when the ladies of the settlement are invited to a splendid ball' (Commentary to *Oriental Scenery*, William and Thomas Daniell). The Assembly Rooms were demolished in the 1970s, although the racecourse remains.

The word gymkhana is virtually synonymous in modern England with enthusiastic young girls and recalcitrant ponies, and sounds as if it has deep roots in British India; the word is in fact a corruption of the Hindi 'gend-khana', a ball house or racket court. It was first used in Bombay in the 1860s, to mean a field where competitive riding and other sports took place.

Horses and horse-breeding were not merely pastimes as far as the Company was concerned, but provided the vital cog in the smooth running of their military and administrative machine. The Company's veterinary surgeon, William Moorcroft, who we first met at the source of the Indus, was in charge of the Company's stud farm at Pusa, Bihar, and the expedition from which he never returned (see page 95) was supposedly one to seek Bukhara ponies. The Company comissioned oil paintings of two of their best horses to hang in East India House in London.

CRICKET

In the history of the British Empire it is written that England has owed her sovereignty to her sports' (J E C Welldon, Bishop of Calcutta and Headmaster of Harrow 1885-98), and if any sport epitomises the legacy of the British in India, it is cricket. Not just a game but a moral code, and to some a virtual religion, cricket was first played in India in 1721 by the officers and men of an English ship. It was adopted enthusiastically in all three of the Company's Presidencies, and the Calcutta Cricket Club was founded in 1792. The Parsees of Bombay were unusually close to the British, both socially and in business, and they formed the Oriental Cricket Club in Bombay in 1848. In the 1880s the British and the Parsees played against each other for the first time; Hindus and Muslims followed suit, and by the twentieth century cricket was well established as the national game.

The rules of cricket became a model for an approach to life; the received virtues of the colonising British were supposed to reflect the gentlemanliness, fair play and good gamesmanship exemplified by the game. It is salutory in this context to note that the rules of the game were first written down in England in order to make gambling on the outcome a more viable prospect among gentlemen, and to help them 'play with the skilled hirelings from the lower classes who acted under their orders' (D Birley, *Sport and the making of Britain*, Manchester University Press, 1993). The underlying aims of cricket, it seems, bore uncanny similarities to the aims of empire.

POLO

It is uncertain whether polo originated in Persia, where the game is recorded from as early as the sixth century, or the Himalayas, where the Balti word for ball, 'pulu', gave its name to the game in English. The Moghuls were certainly playing the game in India by the thirteenth century, and it was considered invaluable for the training of cavalry. They named it 'chaugan', or horse ball, and from the deviousness of their play we derive the word 'chicanery'.

It is likely that polo was first observed by servants of the Company in the Manipur district near Burma, and played in the 1840s by British tea planters who had been encouraged by the Company to settle in Assam. It was introduced a few years later to Calcutta, where it quickly became popular among cavalry regiments at the Calcutta

Hong Kong Races
Start of the Celestials !' Feb 12 20

Polo Club; they in turn brought it back to Britain, where the first game was played at Hurlingham in 1869. The Silchar Club, the world's first polo club, was founded near Manipur in 1859.

Polo was also played in another area of the Himalayas, Baltistan, on the high reaches of the upper Indus. The game is still played there and in neighbouring Ladakh, Hunza, Gilgit and Chitral, in the frenetic local style described by Company surveyors in the 1830s. The quality of the polo ponies bred there is renowned.

The game is also described as being played in Japan, in Chamberlain's *Things Japanese* (3rd edn, London 1898), and by some unknown quirk of fate, the Japanese used a polo stick which matched exactly a description written nearly a millennium earlier of a Persian polo stick.

GOLF AND OTHER GAMES

There were Scotsmen in every rank of the East India Company's armies in India, and the increasing interest of these men in the game of golf led to the founding in 1829 of the oldest golf club outside the British Isles – the Royal Calcutta Golf Club. As the *Oriental Sporting Magazine* remarks: 'We congratulate them on the prospect of seeing that noble and gentleman-like game established in Bengal.' It was originally named the Dumdum Golfing Club, after the barrack town outside Calcutta where the officers were stationed; Dum Dum was also the name given to the infamous expanding bullet.

Again as a result of the Scots presence in the Company's ranks, the Royal Bombay Golf Club followed in 1842, and a shilling, compared to the old 'feathery' (cowhide stuffed with feathers) which cost half a crown (two shillings and sixpence). By 1850, the gutty had prevailed.

A latecomer to the India scene, having become popular in England in the 1850s, croquet was well suited to the climate and milieu of the subcontinent, involving as it did vicious tactics, languid pottering around immaculately manicured lawns, and the participation of both sexes. After the Company's demise, the Viceroy could be seen playing with a solid ivory mallet.

Lawn tennis, supposedly the most popular participation sport in the world, stems from an invention of one Major Walter Wingfield, an officer in the Dragoons who was sent to India during the Mutiny, but had a peaceful posting in Bangalore, where he got married and saw the game of badminton being played. (Badminton may itself have been invented at Badminton, home of the Duke of Beaufort, by officers on leave from India – certainly its first official rules were published in Poona in 1870.) Wingfield realised that badminton could be adapted for outdoor play, using a rubber ball. The game quickly achieved great popularity in England, and although it evolved subsequently, remains largely as Wingfield originally conceived it.

The rise in popularity of the game of rugby came after the East India Company finally reverted to the Crown in 1874, but the game was played in the 1850s by the pupils of Haileybury College, the school owned and run by the Company to educate and prepare boys for Company service. As a result, when those former pupils arrived in India, they took their interest in rugby with them.

The Calcutta Rugby Club was formed in 1872, but it struggled for survival and was disbanded in 1877. When the defunct club offered to present the Rugby Union in England with a cup for a knock-out tournament, it was proposed that the cup should instead be given to the winners of the England versus Scotland international, then in its eighth year. The 'Calcutta Cup', which was made in India from 700 silver rupees of the East India Company, was first played for in 1879, and remains one of the most prestigious trophies in the rugby world. In 1926, the Rugby Union presented the by then re-formed Calcutta Rugby Club with a cup for an All India Competition.

Hockey was known in mediaeval England, and introduced to India by the army. It was adopted by Christian Eurasians, many of whom later came to work for the Indian railways, which accounts for the strength of the railway hockey teams.

The start of the Celestials, Hong Kong's most presitigious horse race.

within twenty years golf clubs had proliferated in other Company territories in the East – Ceylon, Hong Kong, Singapore and Java. The oldest tournament after the British Open and Amateur Championships was the Amateur Championship of India and the Far East, inaugurated by the Royal Calcutta Club in 1892, beating the American equivalent by three years.

Perhaps the greatest single contribution to the development of the game has a more subtle relationship to India. In 1845, a clergyman in St Andrews, Scotland, received a gift of a statue of Vishnu from India. The merits of the statue are not known, but the doctor patented a golf ball made from the gutta-percha in which it was packed. These 'gutties' cost

CONSOLIDATION

> *'Great Empires are not made by seeing the other fellah's point of view!'*
>
> Anon

THE CHURCH AND THE MISSIONARY

Sir Anthony Sherley's *Trauelles* of 1601 amply illustrates contemporary ideas concerning religious toleration: '. . . [their] whole behaviours in point of civilitie (besides that they are all damned Infidels and Zodomiticall Mahomets) doe answer the hate we chriftians doe justly holde them in. For they are beyond all measure the most insolent superbous and insulting people ever more prest to offer outrage to any christian,' he declares, referring to the Arabs of Arabia Felix, now Yemen. The book pauses long enough from this breathless tirade to make the first reference in the English language to 'coffe'.

Warren Hastings (see page 99), by contrast, held characteristically liberal views concerning religious tolerance. Of the Hindu he said it was the duty of the English 'to protect their (the Indians') persons from wrong and to leave their religious creed to the Being who has so long endured it and who will in his own time reform it.' He had no doubts about the superiority of his own creed; he merely forbore to impose it.

Although the Company had since its foundation officially espoused the Protestant faith, its servants were by no means the fiercely proselytising Christians that their predecessors in the East, the Portuguese, had been; whilst encouraging Protestant worship, the Company shrewdly banned any missionary activities on its territories until 1813. Nonetheless, the Church was an important part of daily life, and in the early years churches were built in all the Indian Presidencies – St Mary's in Madras, St John's in Calcutta (replacing a church inconsiderately destroyed by Siraj-ud-dualah), and St Thomas's in Bombay – and, as the Company expanded its operations and pushed further inland, new towns built their own. If nothing else, the churches had churchyards, which meant that the Company had some-where to bury their dead, which the climate, disease and war provided in spectacular numbers; graves were topped by monuments carved in England and shipped as ballast on the lightweight voyage east.

The change in the attitude of the Company to missionaries in 1813 was forced upon them by the success of the Evangelical movement at home. In part, this was reaction to the success of Britain's colonising efforts and domination of the seas, which had brought millions of 'heathens' around the world under their sway and exposed the iniquities of the slave trade to full public scrutiny. Once allowed in, missionaries in India made some headway in 'preaching, teaching and healing', their chosen way to the heathen heart, but there was never the expected wholesale acceptance of the 'superior' religion. Early missionaries believed, with some justification, that the overt sexuality of some Hindu religious symbolism was too much for the delicate sensibilities of the English: the lingam and yoni were flagrantly the male and female genitals, and the temple dancing girls were prostitutes. Hook-swinging (see page 107), a subject of much morbid fascination to the Europeans, particularly outraged the missionaries, but the best they could achieve was to get it banned from taking place near European houses.

By the end of the Company's raj, missionaries had belatedly come to believe in conciliation, not anathematisation, though in truth the debate was never satisfactorily resolved between those who believed the best way to bring Christianity to the heathens was through education, reason and understanding, and those who believed in delivering the message to any who would listen, dispensing rice as a catalyst to enlightenment.

Meanwhile, the Company supported the established Church and contributed substantially to the building of a new cathedral in Calcutta, St Paul's, which was consecrated in 1847 with Bishop Wilson's ominous words, 'It claims India as the Lord's'.

The tolerant attitude of Hastings would not have passed muster with the Evangelical movement, which had done sterling work in the suppression of the slave trade but contributed through its missionary zeal to making the possibility of cordial relations between the Company and its Indian subjects yet more remote. When William Wilberforce, that

A view of Calcutta in the early 1850s, with a fine classical house in the foreground.

A group of Buddhist nuns in Tibet, early 1900s. Tibet had remained closed to all but the most intrepid explorers until this time.

hero of the Abolitionist movement, said 'The Hindu Divinities are absolute monsters of lust, injustice, wickedness and cruelty. In short, their religious system is one grand abomination,' he was expressing a sense of spiritual superiority which dripped down to the temporal realm and, when combined with the domestic travails of the memsahib, reinforced by the Church, led to the apartheid attitudes of the club mentality. By the time of the Mutiny, Hindu and Muslim alike shared a real fear that not just their lands but their core religious beliefs were under threat.

SUTTEE AND THUGGEE

Although the attitude of the Company to the native religions remained largely tolerant, two Hindu practices were proscribed during their time. Suttee, the self-immolation of widows on the funeral pyres of their husbands, was, and still is, highly controversial. By the time of its nominal abolition in 1829 it was almost universally regarded by the English as a hideous practice, but early travellers had more recent memories of Christian martyrs: 'I said to myself, "Why should I think that this woman has done wrong? She had done this to obtain Heaven and God's favour; and have not the great and most learned men in England and other Christian countries done the same to gain Heaven and God's favour, who had the Bible to direct them?", (John MacDonald, *Memoirs of an 18th Century Footman*, Century, 1985). The majority of widows who did not commit suttee had little to look forward to, as their status, freedom and financial support were reduced to virtually nil.

Thuggee was the most violent of the Hindu cults that the Company felt called upon to deal with. Knowing no social divide, Thugs were adherents of Kali, the goddess of Destruction. High on a sacred narcotic concoction, they preyed upon travellers in the winter season across north India, strangling them with a length of cloth in ritual killing grounds, dividing their possessions among themselves, and hiding the bodies. They caused great fear, and it was difficult

An heroic treatment of a widow's suttee by Johann Zoffany, c. 1811.

to find out anything about the victims, let alone the perpetrators of the crimes. It fell to Captain William Sleeman, head of the Department of Thuggee and Dacoity (banditry), to hunt them down, and by 1840 he declared his work almost complete. He undertook a final tour of the previously affected areas with his heavily pregnant wife, who went into labour as they travelled and produced a baby boy. They later learnt that the grove of trees that their carriages had pulled into was a ritual killing ground of the Thugs. Perhaps Kali had the last word.

EDUCATION

At the beginning of the nineteenth century, the Company embarked on a new programme of education for those in its service. Wellesley set up the College of Fort William in Calcutta, and the accomplishments expected from its pupils illustrate the extent to which the Company took its responsibilities in India seriously: ' . . . I would lead your attention to three branches of study; viz. a scientific and grammatical knowledge of the eastern languages that I would class thus as to utility, Arabic, Persian, Hindoostanee, Sanscrit, Bengalee etc. A personal intercourse with natives of all denominations and castes, to acquire idiom, dialect, manner, local knowledge, knowledge of custom, character, prejudice, religion, internal arrangement, ancient hereditary habits, and distinguishing characteristics. A constant conversation and intercourse with . . . those who are remarkable as classical oriental scholars' (William Fraser to his younger brother Alexander, *Fraser Papers,* National Register of Archives, Scotland).

The College provided an excellent grounding for the Company's servants, but it was Wellesley's more far-sighted successor, Lord Hastings, who suggested that education

St John's Church, Calcutta, 1838.

might provide the means for England 'to enlighten her temporary subjects'. The Vidyalaya was founded in 1817 to promote the education of Indians in western literature and science, and, under Governor General William Bentinck, other schools and colleges were set up by the Company for the teaching of English – considered 'the key to all improvements'. Thomas Babington Macaulay, one of the most able administrators of the last years of the Company, was of the unfortunate opinion 'that a single shelf of a good European library was worth the whole native literature of India and Arabia'.

The ubiquity of the English language among the higher echelons of the native Indians is seen today is some quarters as the final insult imposed by a colonialist oppressor; it was also the instrument by which the constitution and the rule of law could be maintained equally throughout the raj. But by their very nature these pan-subcontinental impositions sowed the seeds of Indian nationalism, fusing disparate interests, cultures and religions into one, albeit alien, construct.

TEA PLANTING AND OTHER COMMERCIAL ENTERPRISES

After the loss of the China monopoly in 1834, the Company had ceased to trade in tea, but had not entirely lost interest in the plant. Sir Joseph Banks' (see page 40) carefully prepared plans for the cultivation of tea on Company territory had not been implemented – apart from a few desultory specimens from China in the Calcutta Botanical Gardens – but the growing and manufacture of tea was well understood in theory by the time that the then Governor General, William Bentinck, took the initiative and formed a Tea

Committee in India in 1834. The existence of wild tea in Assam was confirmed, and by careful cross-breeding of these with Chinese tea plants and the use of experienced Chinese labour, the Company was able to send the first twelve chests of Assam tea to auction in London in 1839. The same year saw the first amateur efforts at cultivation by Dr Cambell, the Company's superintendent in the newly acquired Darjeeling district, which produced tea of a quality still pre-eminent today, as well as the first plantings in the botanical gardens at Peradeniya in Ceylon (Sri Lanka). Ceylon was largely given over to coffee, but when the plantations were devastated by 'coffee rust' in the 1860s, the tea plants became an invaluable substitute. In India, private firms such as the East India Tea Company and the Assam Company developed plantations in the 1840s and, not without headaches and near disasters, laid the foundations of the phenomenal growth of the Indian tea industry. They were assisted by the Company-sponsored mission into Bohea, China, by Robert Fortune, who returned in 1851 with seeds and detailed observations of tea-growing there. By the time of the Mutiny, Indian tea exports scarcely register in the statistics, but only twenty years later they had overtaken those of China.

One of the Company's indigo factories in operation in Bengal.

The growing of opium (see page 172) was commercially very successful, and the cultivation of indigo plants continued as it had done from ancient times. The industrialisation of the native jute cultivation was encouraged by Scottish entrepreneurs from Dundee, and matured into a substantial trade as the demand for 'gunny' bags for agricultural commodities multiplied around the world. Bulk export commodities included saltpetre for the manufacture of gunpowder, indigo, hemp, salt, and opium.

Some aspects of Indian industry suffered badly under the Company in later years. With Indian imported cotton and silk selling profitably at half the price of comparable goods of home manufacture, the English cloth industry successfully lobbied for the imposition of swingeing import duties to enable the Lancashire mills to keep turning. India, being under the control of the Company, was in no position to retaliate by imposing duties on English goods coming into India. This more insidious form of colonialist corruption was noted at the time: the success of the English textile industry was 'created by the sacrifice of Indian manufactures. Had India been independent, she (by retaliatory duties) would thus have preserved her own productive industries from annihilation. This act of self-defence was not permitted to her; she was at the mercy of the stranger. British goods were forced on her without paying any duty; and the foreign manufacturer employed the arm of political injustice to keep down and ultimately strangle a competitor with whom he could not contend on equal terms.' (Professor H H Wilson in James Mill, *History of India*, 1845).

ABOLITION, ARABS AND AFRICA

The Abolitionist movement made itself felt late in India. Thomas Babington Macaulay, architect of much of the Indian legal code, was again a key figure, drawing up a bill abolishing slavery through the territories of the Indian Government, which was passed in 1843. This proved an embarrassment in Zanzibar, where Sultan Seyyid Said, the ruler of a war-torn Muscat, had set up court, and was making a very tidy living out of the slave trade, under the nose of the appointed East India Company official, Captain Atkins Hammerton. The East India Company regarded East Africa as lying within its sphere of influence, resisting any attempts of the government in London to meddle in the affairs of the 'English lake', and the development of the steamship route between Suez, Bombay and beyond had reinforced the patrician attitude that

it had developed towards Arabian and East African affairs; there was even talk of the Company taking a territorial interest in East Africa — a raj within a raj. Gifts of a cannon and guns were sent to Sahle Selassie, King of Ethiopia, and the explorers Richard Burton and John Hanning Speke, both dyed-in-the-wool India hands, were partly sponsored by the Company on their exploration of the unknown African interior. With 'Doctrine-of-Lapse' Dalhousie at the helm in India it was almost conceivable that the Company might take on Africa. The Mutiny put paid to that.

INFRASTRUCTURE AND ADMINISTRATION

The Company had minted its own coins from the late seventeenth century; initially, the currency was only one among a welter of coins from around the world which were used for trade. Later, as the Company's commercial and territorial reach expanded, its currency was to achieve a high level of acceptance and this greatly simplified trading transactions.

Apologists for empire always point to the remarkable infrastructure projects undertaken in India as examples of the good the English brought, yet, whilst the map of the Company's territory in India at the start of the nineteenth century was expanding hourly, on the ground conditions were frequently difficult. William Fraser, posted to Delhi as assistant to the Resident, took six months to get there by boat and road from Calcutta in 1805: 'the country is still infested with robbers and plunderers, people cannot travel unattended. Five or six troopers are sufficient protection' (*Fraser Papers*, Bundle 439, National Register of Archives, Scotland).

Most infrastructural improvements came after the Company had left, but some were built during their time, and remarkable they certainly were. Recognising the need for efficient transport and good roads, the Company created a metalled road from Bombay to Calcutta, as well as undertaking a spectacular refurbishment of the old Grand Trunk Road — a vital thread in Kipling's *Kim* — which ran for 1,500 miles from Calcutta to Peshawar on the Northwest Frontier. The Ganges canal was built for irrigation — at the time the largest civil engineering project on the planet, involving a canal system 2,800 miles long.

Railways, too, made their first appearance under the Company, with the first twenty miles opening in 1853 between Thana and Bombay, and a line following the route of the Grand Trunk Road following thereafter.

The Writers' Building in Calcutta. Although extensively remodelled, it is still in use today.

As the Company started to control territories in India, so the administration of its nascent raj became increasingly important. The writers, who previously would have recorded the day-to-day commercial transactions of the factory, found themselves accounting for the tax revenues of an entire province such as Bengal. Such rapid changes, daunting as they may have been, made the Company's expansion in India the challenge that attracted so many to it.

The exclusion of Anglo-Indians from the Company's service from the beginning of the nineteenth century was echoed by a yet more draconian exclusion of native Indians. Half a century before, Warren Hastings had foreseen and condemned this short-sighted policy: 'I hope that neither the present nor any future administration will think of committing inferior detail to the control of a British subject. To establish them in this world would be to subvert the rights of the family, to injure the revenues, and to loosen the attachment of the peasants which it will ever be good policy to conciliate.'

When the Company lost its trading monopolies in favour of government in India, the Indian Civil Service (I C S) grew to be one of the most prestigious and uncorrupt administrations of its kind anywhere in the world. The entrance examinations were formidably difficult, and the elite body of the I C S attracted men of the highest calibre – a standard that was maintained after Independence.

COMPANY IN TROUBLE

> '...all plan and purpose incarnate, without any
> superfluous humanity'.
>
> Rabindranath Tagore, 1922

THE INVASION OF AFGHANISTAN

The fears of a Russian invasion of India prompted the name the 'Great Game' for the espionage activities of both sides in the high Himalayas, though in fact this belongs more properly to the era after the Company had left. Yet there were a number of precursors to this cold war, and undercover expeditions into the virtually unknown regions north of Afghanistan were mounted with mixed success. The hero of one such expedition, Alexander 'Bukhara' Burnes, reported from Kabul to the Russophobic Governor General, Lord Auckland, that Russian envoys were making significant progress with Dost Mohammed, ruler of Afghanistan; in fact, the Khan wanted to ally himself with the Company against the Sikhs, who, under the command of Ranjit Singh, had taken Peshawar and were pressing hard towards the Khyber Pass. Lord Auckland was panicked into mounting a full-scale invasion of Afghanistan to place, in the time-honoured tradition, a compliant claimant, Shah Shuja, on the throne. Never mind that Dost Mohammed was a strong and capable ruler who had united his country, and Shah Shuja was weak and cruel; the perceived Russian threat had to be firmly countered.

The invasion of 1838 reflected the mood of the Company: seemingly invincible, the English lion needed only to stretch out a paw for kingdoms to tremble before it. But Afghanistan was another kind of country; unruly, harsh, and peopled by tribes of proud, brave fighting men who

Mutineers being dramatically 'blown away' from guns by Europeans out for revenge.

CHAPTER XVI

Central Asian traders gather to buy and sell their wares outside the city of Kabul in 1840.

were to win the grudging admiration of the English through to Independence, and who, in turn, respected the English fighting spirit above all others.

Initially, all went according to plan, and the Army of the Indus, some 13,000 strong, with the usual retinue of camp-followers and packs of fox hounds, made stately progress through Sind and over the Bolan Pass towards Kabul. Fierce fighting broke out at Ghazni, but by August 1839 Dost Mohammed had fled Kabul and Shah Shuja was installed on the throne.

The English complacently settled in, installing those essentials of a civilised frontier life – a racecourse and bibis. The latter caused great offence to the fiercely Muslim tribal 'Afghans, who were not accustomed to their womenfolk being treated with such disrespect. The magazine and armoury were cunningly placed away from the main camp; and the bulk of the army departed, leaving a smaller force to prop up Shah Shuja.

For two years they remained, at a cost of over a million pounds a year, with no perceivable benefit to the Company, then disaster struck. Burnes, the Resident, was murdered in the bazaar and the country rose up in revolt. With incompetent leadership, an indefensible position, and attacked by the fiercest warriors in Asia, Kabul, together with Shah Shuja and his hundred-strong harem, was abandoned. The retreat from Kabul of the Army of the Indus in the winter of 1842 is one of the most bloody in British military history. Over 16,500 men, women and children – 4,500 soldiers, sepoys and cavalry and 12,000 camp followers – made their way, freezing and half-starved, across the mountainous road

leading to Jelalabad and safety. All were slaughtered, captured or enslaved, with exception of Dr Brydon, who survived to tell the grim news to the garrison at Jeladabad.

The destruction of the Army of the Indus did untold damage to the myth of the Company's invincibility in India, and caused much soul-searching back home. A church was erected in Bombay, where most of the Army had been based, with the names of the fallen officers and NCOs carved in the chancel walls.

THE OPIUM TRADE AND WAR WITH CHINA

If there is one aspect of the Company's trade which is regarded as irredeemably venal today, it is the opium trade. The received wisdom goes as follows: in the early part of the nineteenth century, the Company, desperately needing silver to pay for Chinese tea, realised that the Chinese themselves would provide the silver in exchange for opium, which the Company grew in India. Exploiting the greed of private traders and the corruption of petty Chinese officials, they contrived to smuggle opium into China covertly, circumventing a Chinese imperial ban on the sale of opium and distancing themselves from the increasing addiction of millions of Chinese to the drug. When the Chinese Emperor threatened to back up the ban with force, the Company, faced with disastrous loss of revenue, sent in the navy in defence of 'free trade'. The Company is thus found guilty of gross moral turpitude, and 'appropriate' lessons are conscientiously drawn concerning the evils of unbridled capitalism, western colonialist hypocrisy, Third World exploitation, and so forth.

A view of the Bala Hissar, the citadel of the Afghanistan capital, in 1840.

Dr Brydon bringing news of the Kabul catastrophe to the garrison at Jelalabad, depicted in Elizabeth Butler's inimitable style.

Needless to say, it was note quite so simple. Opium had been used in different parts of the world since ancient times, principally as a soporific, and laudanum, a tincture of opium in alcohol, was widely used for fevers and other malaises – less commonly, as an inspiration to poetry (without it, Kubla Khan's 'stately pleasure-dome' might never have been decreed). In England, the cultivation of opium was encouraged, and the Royal Society of Arts Manufactures and Commerce had awarded a gold medal to Mr Young, a Scottish surgeon, for his remarkable efforts which produced a profit of £117 6s an acre – the fact that he also claimed to have extracted opium from lettuces aroused no suspicion. Within this context, it was natural that the Company should experiment with its cultivation in India, which proved capable of producing opium of higher quality than that of either Turkey or Persia, the two principal existing sources.

Opium had been used in China since the early seventeenth century, and was smoked mixed with tobacco. It was the latter that attracted most opprobrium, and selling it was made a capital offence. When an imperial edict of 1729 banned the sale of opium itself, the Company issued orders to its ships' commanders not to carry it to China, 'as you will answer to the Honourable Company on your peril'. However, in China itself the edict was generally ignored, and in the 1770s a French traveller reported that the Chinese had developed 'an unbelievable passion for this narcotic'.

The Company took charge of opium production in India from 1781, and sold it at auction in Calcutta to private traders. Officially, the Company had no notion of its destination; in reality, they knew full well, and the quantity exported in this way to China rose from a thousand to four thousand chests of about 150 lbs a year. New edicts in China banned opium absolutely, but 'there was no pretence at enforcing them in the spirit' and 'irregular dues' were levied to ensure the connivance of the 'Hoppo, Viceroy, Governor, Treasurer, and so on down the list' (Morse, *Chronicles of the East India Company Trading to China,* London, 1926–9, vol ii).

Lord Macartney had been briefed to tackle the problem of the opium trade in his 1793 Embassy to China; the Company wisely acknowledged that nothing should be allowed to put its vital tea trade in jeopardy, and 'useful as the opium revenue was to India, it was less to be desired than the China trade monopoly'. His failed mission left the issue unresolved, and the level of trade remained the same until the 1830s; it represented under 5 per cent of the Company's annual Indian revenues – significant, but scarcely vital.

After 1830 consumption rose dramatically and the Company suddenly realised the extent to which it had become quietly hooked on opium revenues. Meanwhile, the Chinese Government was debating that perennial issue of prohibition versus legalisation, and private traders were gloomily predicting that the legalisers would win the argu-

John Nicholson

One of the veterans of the First Afghan War, John Nicholson, went on to carve a formidable career for himself as another Lion of the Punjab, under Sir Henry Lawrence. He was extremely effective in the unruly tribal territories bordering Afghanistan, where he kept the mummified head of a notorious bandit on his desk, to inspire fear. He flogged miscreants and hanged malefactors, but tempered his ferocity with acts of extraordinary mercy; the Sikhs were so impressed when he told all his prisoners after the Battle of Gujerat in 1849 to go quietly home, that a sect of 'Nikkulseynites' sprang up, revering him as the reincarnation of Bramha. Fakirs flogged themselves in his honour (flogging seems to have been a recurrent theme in his life) and two killed themselves on hearing news of his death. A large man with a brooding presence, inarticulate and scarcely literate, adored by his soldiers and respected by his peers, he was the Victorian ideal, the muscular Christian personified, and his apotheosis came with his heroic death at the siege of Delhi. The Nikkolseyn cult survived through to the turn of the century, and to this day his monolithic memorial looms over the Grand Trunk Road near Rawalpindi.

An opium den in Chinatown, London. Chinese sailors carried their addiction with them.

ment; in the event, the Emperor took his strongest action yet – a total clampdown on the opium trade in 1837. Cantonese opium dealers were strangled in front of the foreign factories *'pour encourager les autres'*, and as the tension escalated, leading Hongs were arrested and stocks ordered to be surrendered; when only token amounts were collected, threats were made against Lancelot Dent, a leading private trader implicated (rightly) in opium smuggling. Captain Elliot, the Crown representative in Canton, who was broadly sympathetic with the ban, ordered the surrender of all opium in private traders' hands. Over a thousand tonnes, valued at £2,000,000, was burnt on the banks of the Pearl river.

It might all have ended there, but a wrangle started over who should pay for the burnt opium; the traders thought that they should be compensated by the Crown, as they were acting on Elliot's orders, and the Crown harboured hopes that the Chinese Government could be prevailed upon to pay. But the Canton Governor, Lin, buoyed up by the apparent ease of his victory over the foreign barbarians, began to ratchet up his demands to an extent that Elliot could not countenance, particularly his insistence that any opium found on board a ship would result in the death penalty for its owner. Although the British Government accepted that the Chinese had a sovereign right to ban opium from its territories, they were not to be forced to the negotiating table, and so, in 1839, three thousand men were sent to make 'war on the master of one-third of the human race'.

The term 'Opium Wars', coined by *The Times,* was a catchy title for a war that certainly concerned the opium trade, but was more about trade in general; there is no evidence that the English fought for the right to impose opium imports on a suppliant Chinese Empire.

The result was that a small army and a small naval fleet, supplemented by some Company steamers, prevailed over a Chinese Empire full of an anachronistic sense of its own importance. Over decades, if not centuries, it had been fragmented and weakened by internal strife and misrule, and was in no condition to resist the terms imposed by the humiliating Treaty of Nanking in 1842, which forced the opening of the 'treaty ports', including Shanghai, to foreign trade, and, most significantly, ceded Hong Kong to the British.

THE BUILD-UP TO THE MUTINY

The Indian Mutiny a.k.a the First War of Independence is still seen as one of the defining moments of the British rule in India. It led to the absorption of the Company by the Crown, further alienated the rulers from the ruled, and sowed the seeds which ultimately led to Independence in 1947.

Mutinies in the various armies in India in the service of the Company or the Crown were by no means unknown: twenty-nine are recorded in the official annals, the most common causes being threat to caste and lack of pay or allowances. The grievances were largely genuine, especially in the case of the sepoy mutinies, of which it was written in 1826, 'I am happy to say that I have not discovered a single instance of the sepoys having shown insubordination or any disposition to mutiny unless when improperly treated' (Captain W Badenach, *Inquiry into the State of the Indian Army,* London, 1828). The sepoys were professional soldiers, and expected professional treatment in return. One of the underlying causes of the Mutiny in 1857 was the almost wilful lack of respect with which the sepoys were increasingly treated: '[the sepoy] is devoted to us yet, but we take no pains to preserve his attachment' (Sir Charles Napier, 1849). Mutiny was a capital offence, and in the worst cases offenders were 'blown away' by guns. This particularly grisly fate, with the victim strapped in front of a cannon and, when it was fired, his blood and body parts splattered over the vengeful onlookers (page 171), was invented by the Moghuls and adopted by the British.

The spark that finally ignited the Mutiny was the issue of cartridges for the new Enfield rifles, supposedly greased with beef fat (to cause maximum offence to Hindus) or pig fat (to offend Muslims), and seen as part of a wider conspiracy to cause religious and caste law to be defiled, preparatory to the installation of compulsory Christianity. Of course this was not the case, but there were sufficient seeds of truth to give rise to such imaginings. On the issue of greased cartridges, a subject which continues to vex historians, it appears that the Company had been unable to obtain sufficient supplies of the Enfield rifles for which the cartridges were required, and quickly reverted to the old Brown Bess smooth-bore muskets when it was realised that there were good grounds for suspecting that the cartridges may well have been greased with beef or pig fat. The cartridges for the smooth-bore muskets, which had been in use for years, had by an unhappy coincidence been changed slightly (the paper had been sourced in Serampore instead of London), and suddenly these in turn were regarded with suspicion by the sepoys. The outbreak at Meerut on 10 May 1857, which signalled the start of the Mutiny, was prompted by the refusal to use the old cartridges. The fact that during the Mutiny the sepoys mainly used these same cartridges which had previously been anathema to them suggests that the cartridge issue was in fact only a small part of a package of grievances.

British troops line up in Canton after their victory in the so-called 'Opium Wars'.

Nevertheless the British, throughout their time in India, had an aptitude for upsetting religious sensitivities. The Commander-in-Chief in Bombay in 1770, General Pimble, was reported by John MacDonald to have imposed an order that Hindu officers under his command should wear leather boots. They complained that to do so would cause them to lose caste and be deprived of the company of their families, and, when he insisted, they resigned. Not that the lesson was learned: the brief mutiny at Velore in 1806 was caused by a new order that sepoys must wear leather cockades in their turbans and remove their caste marks. Brahmin sepoys were also dismayed to find that as a result of changes in the regulations they might be posted overseas – a sea voyage was against caste law. However, the Indian army would not have functioned if its officers had continually upset caste or religious sensitivities, and there were genuine efforts to accommodate differences: festivals were observed, eating and drinking requirements respected, and by the 1840s Hindu priests were to be found doing what a padre in a European regiment would do, such as blessing the regimental colours.

Other factors played their part. Resentment was also caused by the so-called Doctrine of Lapse, initiated by Lord Dalhousie in 1848. It was the custom in the by-now semi-independent Indian states for a ruler without a natural heir to adopt one – if for no other reason than that, under Hindu doctrine, a son, whether natural or adopted, must perform the funeral rights for his father. Dalhousie decreed that where a ruler had no natural heir, the Company would take over on his death. This resulted in a swift expansion of the Company's territories and revenues, but left a number of embittered, dispossessed heirs in places such as Oudh and Jhansi, for whom the Mutiny became a natural outlet for their grievances. In the Army, many regiments were dismayed when allowances previously payable for a 'foreign' posting were reduced as the annexation of these states proceeded apace.

Dalhousie enacted other, more liberal statutes: one enabled converts from any religion to enjoy full rights of inheritance; another removed the legal obstacles to a Hindu widow remarrying. Both reflected a social sophistication and lofty idealism, but they had the effect of undermining traditional ideas and fuelling suspicions of a coming compulsory Christianisation.

The old system of officering regiments with a few, well qualified Europeans, whilst allowing Indian soldiers to rise to positions of responsibility, had given way to one in which preferment depended on seniority rather than capability, and the European officers, as well as having their discretionary powers considerably curtailed, were frequently superannuated has-beens; meanwhile, the more capable and ambitious young bloods were siphoned off into the burgeoning civil service.

The memsahib was also blamed for indirectly precipitating the Mutiny, but, ironically, it may have been the result of the actions of a memsahib 'gone sour', a white woman born in India named Mees Dolly, madame of a house of ill-repute in the Meerut bazaar. When eighty-five sepoys were court-martialled and imprisoned for refusing to use the greased cartridges, Dolly and her girls refused their favours to the other sepoys. 'We have no kisses for cowards,' they sneered. Thus spurned, the sepoys broke into the gaol and set their comrades free. Mees Dolly may have sparked off the Mutiny, but if the story is true, she almost certainly saved the raj, for historians are broadly agreed that mutiny across the whole of north India was being planned to coincide with a hundred years of British rule, and the premature outbreak at Meerut disrupted the strategy. Despite this inadvertent contribution to the future British Empire, Mees Dolly was unceremoniously hanged for 'egging on the mutineers'.

Another story concerning the lead-up to the Mutiny which has proved of enduring popular appeal concerns chapatis. Like their descendants which grace the tables of Indian restaurants around the world today, chapatis were flat, round breads – although at that time only a couple of inches across. In the weeks leading up to the Mutiny, senior British civil servants and military officers right across north India kept finding little piles of these chapatis in odd places, such as on verandah steps or under a pile of papers on a desk. Nobody seemed to know where they came from or what they meant, and they left a disquieting sense of trouble brewing. History has offered no adequate explanation of this baffling 'chapati running', and there appears to be no identifiable figure or organisation behind the affair, but current thinking suggests that it was a subtle form of psychological warfare which may have involved chaukidars (watchmen) at police stations. They would pass chapatis to colleagues who would, in turn, pass others on to their counterparts in neighbouring villages, even obtaining receipts. Students of oriental magic will be pleased to hear that the mysterious chapati curse lives on; an attempt in 1997 by a British climber to scale a Himalayan peak unaccompanied was abandoned when he bit into a chapati and flour blew into his face, causing him to sneeze violently and strain his back. The peak that foiled him, Nanga Parbat, is said by locals to be home to fairies, giant frogs and snow snakes a hundred feet long.

DRAMATIC EVENTS

A telegram from Kate Moore in Meerut to her father in Agra, sent at 9.00 pm on 10 May 1857 read: 'The cavalry have risen, setting fire to their own houses and several officers' houses, besides having killed and wounded all the European soldiers and officers they could find near the lines. If aunt intends starting tomorrow evening, please detain her from doing so, as the van has been prevented from leaving the station' (*Papers relating to the Indian Mutiny*, vol 1 of 6, London, 1858).

The telegram highlights the particular drama of the Mutiny: death and destruction amid the ordered domestic life of the cantonment.

The Mutiny engulfed most of northwest India for the best part of a year, and featured numerous atrocities, massacres, battles, skirmishes and much personal loss and heroism. Two incidents fire the contemporary and the modern imagination alike: the massacre at Cawnpore and the Siege of Lucknow. Some two hundred European women and children of the Cawnpore cantonment were tricked by the dastardly Nana Sahib into taking shelter in the notorious

bibigurh, where they were slaughtered in a manner sufficiently brutal to tax even the imaginations of patriotic Victorian leader writers. That Nana Sahib always protested his innocence, and, before the Mutiny, was friendly with the British, had attended the local Masonic lodge and acquired a creditable game of billiards, has been generally ignored by both British and Indian historians alike — by the former, as it undermined his status as arch-villain; by the latter because it undermined his status as arch-patriot. The lack of consensus between the views of the victors and the oppressed is no surprise, but there is a certain lack of magnanimity in the replacement in recent times of the Cawnpore Memorial, built by the British over the well where the hapless victims were thrown, with a bust of Tantia Topi, Nana Sahib's general.

'Remember Cawnpore! Remember the ladies!' became the battle cry of the British troops fighting the sepoys during the Mutiny, and was used to justify the most appalling brutality against equally innocent, but non-European, civilians. Dark rumours circulated that the women had been raped, but 'There is not a particle of credible evidence of the poor women having been "ill-used" anywhere,' wrote the sensible Lady Canning (wife of Charles, Lord Canning, Governor General during the Mutiny) in a letter to Queen Victoria. That did not prevent the popular press from whipping up a sentimental hysteria for revenge: 'Make the hoarse thunder of our guns sweet music in our ears and darken even the heart's devotion, until their wrongs shall be

Hong Kong

The defeat of the Chinese provided the opportunity for the British to force the secession of Chinese territory, not in pursuit of imperial expansion as in India, but for trade. The experience leading up to the Opium Wars had forcibly reminded the British Crown and the private trading interests that Canton was by no means a secure location, and the search for such a base, which had been intermittently carried on for as long as the Company

had traded with China, resumed. During the war, Captain Elliot had sheltered from a Chinese attack in the harbour of Hong Kong island, and was convinced of its suitability, although Formosa, Amoy and Chusan were also considered. In the event, Hong Kong was chosen, and although it was never a Company territory, it was a logical extension of the Company's involvement in China over many years.

The remains of the Residency at Lucknow after the siege during the Mutiny of 1857.

avenged.' (*Illustrated London News*, 1857). The paper printed a picture of Nana Sahib which was (as was probably well known by the paper at the time) in fact that of Ajodhya Prasad, a wealthy banker from Meerut who had presented the portrait to his London lawyer. His undeserved notoriety spread throughout the subcontinent when this picture was used on a 'wanted' poster for the fleeing Nana Sahib.

The western press surpassed themselves in the vilification of the wretched Butcher of Cawnpore. One French periodical came up with a peculiarly refined description of his barbarity: he was said 'to read Balzac, play Chopin on the piano and, lolling on a divan and fanned by gorgeous Kashmiri girls, to have a roasted English child brought in occasionally on a pike for him to examine with his pince-nez' (quoted in P J O Taylor, *Chronicles of the Mutiny*, HarperCollins India, 1992).

Another story put about to inspire the troops was that Miss Ulrica Wheeler, the daughter of the Commanding General at Cawnpore, had been kidnapped by a sepoy, whose head she cut off as he slept, adding those of his family for good measure, before throwing herself down a well. Poems were written and illustrated, commemorating her bravery and honour, and her heroic tale steeled English resolve. However, in 1907, a doctor in Cawnpore was summoned to the deathbed of an elderly lady – Ulrica Wheeler – who told the doctor that she had lived happily married to the sepoy who had rescued her from the slaughter at Cawnpore, and now wished for a Christian absolution.

The Siege of Lucknow was an 'epic of the race', full of dramatic events and the source of many enduring stories and legends. Englishmen *in extremis* were supposed, of course, to share everything regardless of rank, remain unflinchingly brave and unshakeably upright. The fortitude of the 3,100 besieged during the hot summer months of 1857 was remarkable, and if there were unseemly squabbles over the allocation from the stores, suicides owing to the shortage of opium for addicted officers, and half could scarcely stand because of the ravages of cholera, such human weakness only heightens the horror of the event.

The siege was relieved twice: the first time, the rescuers merely joined the defenders; the second time, a column of British reinforcements under the command of Sir Colin Campbell succeeded in lifting the siege after nearly three months. Havelock, commander of the first relief column, died of dysentery and was promptly commemorated by a statue in Trafalgar Square.

Whilst the Siege of Lucknow was reported in gory detail, and its survivors treated as heroes, life for those mutineers themselves besieged by the English in Delhi has received scant attention. The fact that the English were more diligent chroniclers, that they had more coherent leadership, but above all that they won, has meant that there is a dearth of contemporary Indian accounts of the Mutiny. At the end, the lame duck King of Delhi, Bahadur Shah II (opposite), tried half-heartedly to flee the city, but turned himself over to his Head of Intelligence, Rajab An, who was in the act of escorting him back to safety when he came across the vainglorious commander of the eponymous Hodson's Horse, who took all the credit for pursuing and apprehending the last of the Moghul Emperors. Hodson sealed this achievement by shooting dead, in cold blood, the Emperor's two sons and grandson, to prevent them being rescued by the onlookers, he claimed. As his biographer Captain Trotter wrote admiringly, 'with a bold disregard of fine sentiment and personal responsibility – that bugbear of all weak minds [he solved] the problem in his own masterful and fearless way' – a breathtakingly self-assured description of an atrocity.

But Hodson's unprincipled behaviour only reflected that of the English in general, who looted the fine old city of Delhi with all the enthusiasm that greed and vengeance could inspire, and women and children were not necessarily spared in the ensuing bloodbath. 'All the people of the city found within the walls when our troops entered were bayoneted on the spot . . . These were not mutineers but residents of the city who trusted to our well-known mild rule of pardon. I am glad to say they were disappointed.' The Mutiny proved one thing about the English to the Indians; 'not that they were worse than those who had gone before, but that they were certainly no better'.

Why, then, did the Mutiny fail? The absence of an identifiable leader with a steadying influence meant the sepoy armies suffered from dramatic mood swings from euphoria to deepest gloom – an attitude unsuited to a long campaign. Technically, the Brown Bess muskets they used were no match for the new Enfield rifles of the English, and they only had round shot for their artillery – useful for battering fortifications, but of little account against infantry. Some gave more complex explanations: Karl Marx and Frederick Engels, who took a lively interest in the rebellion, ascribed its failure to the betrayal of Indian nationalism by an entrenched feudal class. The success of the Company in retaining its possessions merely highlighted the importance and the vulnerability of India to the Crown: to the East India Company, inevitably, the Mutiny meant the end.

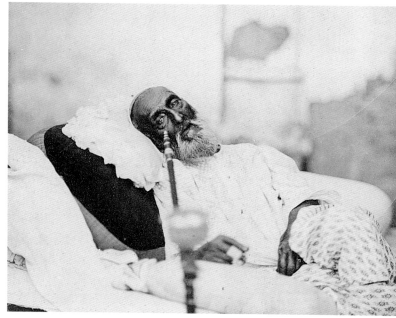

Muhammed Bahadur Shah Zafar, the last of the Moghul Emperors, 1857.

Relieved English after the second relief of Lucknow – the first merely provided reinforcements.

COMPANY OUT

> *'Let her Majesty appreciate the gift — let her take the vast country and the teeming millions of India under direct control; but let her not forget the great corporation from which she has received them.'*
> Statement of the East India Company Court of
> Directors, 1 September 1858

The Company could not survive the Mutiny. What had been a pragmatic, makeshift anomaly now became a political liability. Its 1,700 stockholders could no longer be allowed to rule, if only on paper, over 'the teeming millions'. The end, when it came, was swift and dignified. The Company fielded its most eloquent servant, John Stuart Mill, to write a measured plea for a stay of execution to the Government, first of Lord Palmerston, then, when that fell, of Lord Derby, which proved unimpressed by Mill's argument that the Company's rule 'has been not only one of the purest in intention, but one of the most beneficent in act, ever known among mankind'. The India Bill was passed on 2 August 1858, and the Company's remaining armies, batteries, churches, colleges, debts, desks, elephants, godowns, graves, judges, lascars, navies, paintings, papers, pensioners, prisoners, powers, treaties, territories, vassals, vessels, warehouses and whorehouses were vested in Her Majesty Queen Victoria.

The last meeting of the full Court of Directors of the 'United Company of Merchants of England trading to the East Indies' was held on the 1 September 1858 at East India House in Leadenhall Street. The occasion produced suitably solemn panegyrics and weighty admonitions to the Queen, who noted privately, and with truly imperial complacency, her pleasure that her subjects felt 'that India should belong to me'.

The change from Company rule to Crown rule was proclaimed throughout the subcontinent on 1 November 1858, accompanied by a public holiday and fireworks, but it is doubtful whether many understood the difference. John Company had always been an elusive character, and the loyalties he had engendered were a measure of the vigour of his actions and the depth of his purse, not of personal merit. Her Majesty Queen Victoria had been his public face for twenty years, and that she had finally usurped his throne caused no great surprise.

The corpse of the once-great Company was laid out at No 1 Moorgate in the City. The government gave £800 a year for a secretary and a clerk to shuffle the last remnants of paperwork around a nondescript office; a few of the Directors met on occasion to determine not a great deal; the last Chairman, Colonel Sykes, died in 1872; in 1873, dividends on East India Company stock ceased to be paid, and the Proprietors received the promised £200 in government stock and securities for every £100 of Company stock that they held. In 1874, the Charter of the Company, which had been renewed in 1854, finally expired. The Company had simply ceased to be, not with a bang, nor even a whimper.

The interests of the East India Company and those of the British Crown had gradually merged, so that by the time of the Company's demise they were more or less indistinguishable. But in the emergent British Empire the imperial style differed where the Company had once held sway.

The Company's aims were never those of outright colonisation; it did not seek to establish permanent settlements of Englishmen abroad, but to impose its rule through tiny, isolated cantonments of English traders, soldiers and administrators. Some of the Company's servants preferred to stay where they were, 'to be buried in a palm-grove within the sound of the surf, and mourned by their progeny of half-bred sons, than face English cold, English haste, and English women', but most were on temporary assignment. The Crown took over the Company's India and it remained the same, but more so; the Company's eastern possessions became Indias in miniature. But the true British colonies of the empire were where white settlers made their home: Australia, Canada, Kenya, Rhodesia.

The vast complexities — political, social, moral and spiritual — that now faced the British and their Empire show how far and fast they had come since the Company's original Charter, with its excited talk of 'Adventures, costs and charges . . . for the increase of our navigation and advancement of trade of merchandise . . . with convenient number of Ships and Pinnaces . . . to the East Indies.'

The Albert Memorial, with Prince Albert studying the catalogue for his pet project, the Great Exhibition of 1851.

The India Hall at the Great Exhibition, 1851, where Tipu's Tiger caused a stir.

From Piracy to Parnassus

The most sensational memorial to the mature imperial sensibility of the English undoubtedly belongs to Prince Albert, Queen Victoria's consort. Rising above the Hyde Park site of the Great Exhibition of 1851 like a gothic space shuttle, Sir Gilbert Scott's Albert Memorial illustrates in sculpture, gilt and mosaic the achievements and ambitions of a nation of once-and-future empire builders. Groups of sculpture at each corner of its plinth represent the continents. The voluptuous female figure symbolising Asia unveils more than just her face atop a prone elephant representing brute force and ignorance subdued; a few fabulously swathed men with turbans, scimitars and fierce expressions ward off strangers, whilst a seated Chinaman guards his tea caddy. Rising above a Parnassus of poets, painters, architects, musicians and sculptors are four large groups representing the acme of high Victorian utilitarianism: Agriculture, Manufacture, Engineering and Commerce, who are busy introducing 'civilization into hitherto uncultivated and barbaric nations'. Higher up still, mosaics in praise of Arts and Sciences are disdained by sculpted angels weary of worldly ambition; others gaze at the globe surmounted, finally, by the cross.

The Imperial View: travellers near Rangoon in 1900, when the Company was a distant memory. V C Scott-O'Connor.

39th

DORSETSHIRE REGIMENT.

This is a Piece of the Regimental Color of the 39th Regiment,
carried at the Battle of Maharajpore, on the
23rd December, 1843, by

ENSIGN THEODORE DAVID BRAY,

Who Fell, mortally wounded, under the fire of the
Maharatta Batteries.

———————

The Regiment was commanded in the Battle by his Father,
LIEUT-COLONEL E. W. BRAY, C.B.,
Who was dangerously wounded.

———————

*The 39th Regiment had nearly 300 Officers, Non-commissioned Officers,
and Privates killed and wounded.*

The legacy

The East India Company was so much part of the warp and weft of history that it is impossible now to pick out one thread and identify it as the Company's particular legacy. The trading houses of the East, Worcestershire Sauce, Lloyds of London, pajamas and the English language all owe much of their global reach to the Company, but it cannot be said they would not have existed without it. Most of the commodities and products which the Company introduced to England are still popular today, such as coffee, tea, porcelain, chutney and chintz, but its 'exports' — cricket, the plantation system, gin, English law — have no less a claim on posterity.

• Opium-growing in Pakistan, the source of much of the world's heroin today, was first encouraged by the Company. Pakistan is also the world's largest producer of cricket balls, footballs and bagpipes.

• Tea consumption in the USA has risen steadily for the last thirty years.

• The export dock of the East India Docks was drained and used for the construction of the 'Mulberry harbour', a floating dock used to considerable effect during the D-Day landings in France in 1944. The site is now an office development, although the original wall has been retained.

• The largest Indian cities are the old Company Presidencies — Bombay, Calcutta and Madras — each of them little more than villages before the Company arrived. Karachi, likewise, is now Pakistan's commercial capital.

• There are six million Protestant Christians living in India, and a million in Pakistan.

• The history of the East India Company is taught in Brazil because of the number of outgoing EastIndiamen that stopped there.

• The Indian, Pakistani and Bangladeshi population in Britain is nearly 750,000. There are more Indian restaurants than any other kind, mostly run by Bangladeshis. Large Indian communities also exist in Canada, Australia and Kenya.

• English is the most widely spoken language in the world. Two recent winners of the prestigious Booker Prize for literature have been of Indian origin, writing in English.

• East India Dock Road and Commercial Road, built by the Company in 1801, at a cost of £10,000, to ease communication between the new East India Dock and the City, are still the key roads into London from the East End.

• Crosby Hall, an early headquarters of the Company (1621-38), was moved stone by stone from Bishopsgate in the City to Cheyne Walk in Chelsea by public subscription at the turn of the century. It was sold without protest in the 1980s by the rump of the Greater London Council to a financier who had been drummed out of Lloyds, the insurance market. Lloyds originated as a coffee house in the 1680s, and its present headquarters are built on the former site of East India House.

• India is the world's largest producer of tea, although home consumption (a habit introduced by the Company) has recently outstripped home production.

• St Helena is a British Crown Dependency. The islanders have no automatic rights of residency in the United Kingdom.

• Afghanistan is among the world's poorest countries and has suffered twenty years of war and internecine strife. It is the only source of good-quality lapis lazuli.

• Singapore remains an independent city state.

• The Royal Armouries house a collection of arms and armour given by the Company; it has relocated from the Tower of London to Leeds in Yorkshire.

• The East India Company has been reborn as a UK plc.

APPENDICES

Original subscribers to the East Indies venture before it received its charter from Elizabeth I in 1600, showing the amount subscribed by each individual

	£
Sir Stephen Soame, Lord Mayor of London	200
Sir John Hart and George Boales	1,000
Sir John Spencer	800
Nicholas Mosley, Alderman	300
Paul Bannyng, Alderman	1,000
Leonard Hallyday, Alderman	1,000
Richard Goddard, Alderman	200
John Moore, Alderman	300
Sir Stephen Soame, Rich. Carter	400
Edward Holmden, Alderman	500
Robert Hampson, Alderman	300
Richard Staper	500
Thomas Symonds	200
John Eldred	400
Robert Coxe, grocer	250
Nicholas Leat, ironmonger	200
Thomas Garway, draper	200
George Holman, grocer	150
Thomas Hiccocke	100
Robert Sandy, grocer	200
Nicholas Pearde, clothworker	100
Thomas Edwardes	200
Nicholas Barnesley, grocer	150
William Dale	100
Nicholas Lyng	100
Nicholas Style, grocer	200
Lawrence Green	200
Edward Collins, clothworker	200
Francis Chery, vintner	200
Oliver Style, grocer	300
Richard and Jason Wyche	200
Thomas and Robert Middleton, Robert Bateman	500
Nicholas Farrer, skinner	200
Francis Terrell	200
Thomas Farrington, vintner	200
Richard Wragge	200
Richard Aldworthe	200
William and Ralfe Freeman	300
William Romney	200
William Paule, George Canvage	300
John Newman, Reinold Greene	200
John Woodward, ironmonger	300
Baptist Hickes, mercer	400
Richard Cockayne and Company	3,000
Clement Mosley, Jerome Suger	250
Richard Stephens	200
Thomas Wheeler, Lawrence Wethrall	200
William Chambers, William Stoane	500
William Aldderley and Thomas Henshawe	300

	£	
Thomas Cambell, Miles Huberd	200	
William Garway, draper	500	
Richard Cocks, grocer	200	
Ralfe Hamor, merchant-tailor	200	
Walter Fletcher	200	
John Robinson, senior, merchant-tailor	200	
Leonard White	200	
Thomas Cordell, mercer	300	
Richard Wiseman, goldsmith	200	
Richard Browne	500	
Roger Owfield	300	
William and Edward Turner	200	
Thomas Cutteler, grocer	200	
Edward Jaymes	200	
Robert Bell, John Potter	200	
John Highlord and John Morris	200	
William and John Gore	300	
Richard Howse and Henry Robinson	200	
Thomas Bostocke, John Ramridge	200	
Roger Howe	200	
William Harrison and William Bonde, merchant-tailor	200	
Robert Lee, alderman	300	
John Buzbridge, James Turner	200	
Urye Babbington	200	
Thomas Smythe, haberdasher	200	
Nicholas Crispe and Comp.	200	
Richard Burrell, grocer	200	
John Hewett	333	6s,8d
John Cornelis, goldsmith	200	
William Hallyday, mercer, John Duckett	200	
Humphrey Wymers, Richard Edmonds	200	
Augustin Skynner, Robert Brooke, Thomas Westwray	300	
Thomas Hines, Robert Barley, Mathew Hamond	300	
Rowland Backhouse Barth and Edward Barnes	400	
Sir Richard Saltonstall and his children	200	
John Coghill, Henry Parkehurste	200	
Thomas Juxon, grocer	200	
Richard Barrett, William Allen, mercer	200	
Thomas Eaton, William Essington	200	
John Cowper, notary	200	
Jason Deane, draper	300	
John Coombe	200	
John Swynerton, junior	300	
Giles Doncombe, Richard Welbye	200	
Edmund Nicholson, grocer	200	
Henry Bridgeman, leather seller	200	
John Suzan, Samuel Garrard	200	
William Barrell, Walter Porter	400	
William Offeley, the elder	200	
John Harbie, skinner	200	
Ralfe Buzbie, grocer	200	
Henry Poalstedd, George Whitmore	200	
Total	**£30,133**	**6s.8d**

Members of the Court of Directors of the Governor and Company of Merchants of London trading into the East Indies, 1600.

Thomas Allabaster
Alderman Paul Bannyng
Robert Bell
William Chambers
Francis Chery
John Combe
Thomas Cordell
John Eldred
William Garraway
William Harryson
John Highelord
Alderman Halliday
Alderman Holweden
Roger Howe
Captain James Lancaster
Nicholas Lynge
John Middleton
Alderman Moore
William Berkley
Robert Sandy
Alderman Thomas Smyth, Governor
Richard Staper
Olyver Style
Richard Wyche
Richard Wyseman

Viceroys and Governors General of India during the Company era

Governors General of Fort William Calcutta, Bengal

1774 – 1785	Warren Hastings
1785 – 1786	Sir John MacPherson (temporary appointment)
1786 – 1793	Lord Cornwallis
1793 – 1798	Lieutenant-General Sir Alured Clarke (temporary appointment)
1798 – 1805	Lord Mornington
1805	Lord Cornwallis (second term)
1805 – 1807	Sir George Barlow
1807 – 1813	Lord Minto
1813 – 1823	Lord Moira
1823	John Adam (temporary appointment)
1823 – 1828	Lord Amherst
1828	Butterworth Bailey (temporary appointment)
1828 – 1834	Lord Bentinck

Viceroys and Governors General of India

1834 – 1835	Lord Bentinck
1835 – 1836	Sir Charles Metcalfe
1836 – 1842	Lord Auckland
1842 – 1844	Lord Ellenborough
1844	William Wilberforce Bird (temporary appointment)
1844 – 1848	Sir Henry Hardinge
1848 – 1856	Lord Dalhousie
1856 – 1868	Lord Canning

Directors of the East India Company between 1758 and 1858

Agnew, Patrick Vans
Alexander, Josais du Pré
Alexander, Henry
Allan, Alexander
Amyand, George
Astell, William Thornton
Astell, John Harvey
Atkinson, Richard
Baillie, John
Bannerman, John Alexander
Baring, Francis
Baron, Christopher
Barrington, Fitzwilliam
Barwell, William
Bayley, William Butterworth
Bebb, John
Becher, Richard
Bensley, William
Boddam, Charles
Boehm, Edmund
Booth, Benjamin
Bosanquet, Jacob
Bosanquet, Richard
Boulton, Henry Crabb
Boyd, John
Browne, John
Bryant, Jeremiah
Burgess, John Smith
Burrow, Christopher
Burrow, Robert
Campell, Archibald M
Campell, Robert
Carnac, James Rivett
Caulfield, James
Chambers, Charles (1)
Chambers, Charles (2)
Cheap, Thomas
Clarke, William Stanley
Clerk, Robert
Cockburn, James
Colebrooke, George
Cotton, John
Cotten, Joseph
Creed, James
Crewicke, Joseph
Cruttenden, Edward Holden
Cuming, George
Currie, Frederick
Cust, Peregrine
Cutts, Charles
Daniell, James
Darell, Lionel
Davis, Samuel
Dempster, George
Dent, William
Dethwick, Thomas
Devaynes, William
Dorrien, John
Drake, Roger
Ducane, Peter
Dudley, George
Dupré, Josias (see 2nd entry)

Eastwick, William Joseph
Edmonstone, Neil Benjamin
Ellice, Russell
Elphinstone, William Fullarton
Ewer, Walter
Farquhar, Robert Townsend
Ferguson, Robert Cutler
Fitzhugh, Thomas
Fletcher, Henry
Forbes, John
Fraser, Simon
Freeman, William George
Galloway, Archibald
Gildart, Richard
Godfrey, Peter
Gough, Charles
Grant, Charles
Gregory, Robert
Hadley, Henry
Hall, Richard
Harrison, John
Harrison, Samuel
Hawkesworth, John
Hogg, James Weir
Hudleston, John
Hunter, John
Hurlock, Joseph
Inglis, Hugh
Inglis, John
Irwin, James
Jackson, John
Jackson, William Adair
James, William
Jenkins, Richard
Johnstone, George
Jones, Robert
Lascelles, Peter
Lemesurier, Paul
Lindsay, Hugh
Loch, John
Lumsden, John
Lushington, James Law
Lushington, Stephen
Lyall, George
Macnaghten, Elliot
Mangles, Ross Donnelly
Manship, John
Marjoribanks, Campell
Marjoribanks, Dudley Coutts
Masterman, John
Melville, William Henry Leslie
Metcalfe, Thomas Theophilus
Michie, John
Millet, George
Mills, Charles (1)
Mills, Charles (2)
Mills, William
Moffat, James
Money, William
Money, W Taylor
Moore, James Arthur
Morris, John
Motteux, John
Muspratt, John Petty
Newhorn, Nathanial
Oliphant, James

Pardoe, John
Parry, Edward
Parry, Richard
Parry, Thomas
Pattison, James
Pattle, Thomas
Peach, Samuel
Peel, Laurence
Philips, Thomas
Pigon, Frederick
Plant, Henry
Plowden, Richard Chicheley
Plowden, W Henry Chicheley
Pollock, George
Prescott, Charles Elton
Prinsep, Henry Thoby
Purling, John
Raikes, George
Ravenshaw, John Goldsborough
Rawlinson, Henry Grewicke
Raymond, John
Reid, Thomas
Robarts, Abraham
Roberts, John
Robertson, Archibald
Robinson, G Abercombie
Rooke, Giles
Rous, Thomas
Rous, Thomas Bates
Rumbold, Thomas
Saunders, Thomas
Savage, Henry
Scott, David (1)
Scott, David (2)
Scrafton, Luke
Seward, Richard
Shank, Henry
Sheperd, John
Smith, George
Smith, Martin Tucker
Smith, John
Smith, Joshua
Smith, Nathaniel
Smith, Richard
Smith, Samuel
Snell, William
Sparkes, Joseph
Stables, John
Stevens, George
Stephenson, John
Stuart, James
Sulivan, Laurence
Sykes, W Henry
Tatem, George
Taylor, John Bladen
Thelusson, G Woodford
Thornhill, John
Thorton, Robert
Thorton, William (1)
Thorton, William (2)
Toone, Sweny
Townson, John
Travers, John
Tucker, Henry St George
Tullie, Timothy
Twining, Richard

Vansittart, Henry
Verelst, Harry
Vivian, John Hussey
Walton, Bourchier
Ward, Edward
Warden, Francis
Warden, Richard
Waters, Thomas
Webber, William
Wheler, Edward
Whiteman, J Clarmont
Wier, Daniel
Wigram, William
Wilkinson, Jacob
Williams, Stephen
Willock, Henry
Willoughby, John Pollard
Wombwell, George
Woodhouse, John
Williams, Robert
Young, William

An account of the amount of all goods sold at the East India Company's auctions from March 1807 to March 1808

Company's Goods	£
Teas	3,795,630
Bengal piece goods	260,307
Coast and Surat piece goods	172,574
Silks	319,212
Pepper	75,839
Saltpetre	179,933
Spice	115,402
Drugs, sugar, coffee etc.	236,957
Private Trade Goods	
Teas	186,193
Piece goods	111,543
Raw silk	253,030
Nankeens	14,037
Pepper	20,066
Saltpetre	337
Drugs, sugar, indigo etc.	2,207,437
Neutral and Prize Property	
Teas	29,269
Drugs, etc.	62,228
Pepper	335
TOTAL	**8,035,389**

PICTURE CREDITS

The author and publishers would like to thank the following individuals and organisations for their kind permission to reproduce photographs:

page 21 Tony Wild; pages 9, 27, 29, 77, 148 National Maritime Museum, London; pages 2, 10, 20, 29, 31, 32, 51, 52 (top & bottom), 53, 54, 55 (bottom), 61, 63, 64, 65 (top), 70, 73, 95, 100, 105, 106, 140 (top), 167, 179 (top) British Library; pages 12, 90, 96 by courtesy of the National Portrait Gallery, London; page 16 reproduced by permission of Birmingham Libraries; pages 22 (top), 23, 25, 35, 41, 43, 44, 45, 57, 69, 93, 94 (bottom), 97 (bottom), 98, 104, 107 (top), 108, 109 (top & bottom), 111, 112, 113, 125, 137, 138 (top & bottom), 153, 182 (top) V&A Picture Library; page 22 (bottom) Cheltenham Art Gallery & Museum/The Bridgeman Art Library; pages 33, 36 (top & bottom), 37, 38, 39 (top & bottom), 46, 55 (top), 56, 59, 62, 75, 83, 85, 103, 114, 115, 116 (top), 117 (top right), 117 (top left), 117 (bottom), 118, 119, 120, 121 (top & bottom), 123, 127, 136, 139, 140 (bottom), 141, 151, 158 (top & bottom), 160, 163, 165, 177, 178 (top), 179 (bottom) Christies Images; pages 42, 135 (top), 164, 183 Royal Geographical Society, London; pages 58, 94 (top), 107 (bottom), 116 (bottom), 131, 132, 133 (top & bottom), 134 (left), 135 (bottom), 147, 157, 171, 172 (bottom), 173, 175 Courtesy of the Director, National Army Museum, London; pages 88, 126, 128, 166 Martyn Gregory Gallery, London; page 97 (top) Crown copyright is reproduced with the permission of the Controller of Her Majesty's Stationery Office; page 143 Getty Images Ltd; page 146 The Flag Institute; page 181 The Telegraph Colour Library; page 182 (bottom) The Bodleian Library, University of Oxford; page 184 by kind permission of Mrs M C Bray.

INDEX